Classics

GLAMORGAN
COUNTY CRICKET CLUB

The crowd swarm onto Sophia Gardens to congratulate the Glamorgan players as they leave the field following their victory over Worcestershire to become County Champions of 1969.

Classics

GLAMORGAN
COUNTY CRICKET CLUB

Best wishes,

ANDREW HIGNELL

TEMPUS

Tempus Publishing Limited
The Mill, Brimscombe Port,
Stroud, Gloucestershire, GL5 2QG

ISBN 0 7524 2182 4

Typesetting and origination by
Tempus Publishing Limited
Printed in Great Britain by
Midway Colour Print, Wiltshire

Also available from Tempus:

100 Greats: Glamorgan CCC	0 7524 1879 3	£12.00
100 Greats: Leicestershire CCC	0 7524 2175 1	£12.00
100 Greats: Northamptonshire CCC	0 7524 2195 6	£12.00
100 Greats: Somerset CCC	0 7524 2178 6	£12.00
100 Greats: Warwickshire CCC	0 7524 2180 8	£12.00
100 Greats: Worcestershire CCC	0 7524 2194 8	£12.00
100 Greats: Yorkshire CCC	0 7524 2179 4	£12.00
Images of Sport: Sussex CCC	0 7524 2192 1	£10.99
Images of Sport: The Australians in England	0 7524 1639 1	£10.99
Lord's: Cathedral of Cricket	0 7524 2167 0	£25.00
A False Stroke of Genius: The Wayne Larkins Story	0 7524 2166 2	£12.99
Turnbull: A Welsh Sporting Legend	0 7524 2182 4	£14.99

Wilf Wooller commentates for BBC Wales as Glamorgan win the 1969 County Championship at Cardiff.

INTRODUCTION

This is a personal selection of fifty of Glamorgan's greatest matches, spanning the club's existence from 1888, initially as a Minor County, and since 1921 as a first-class county in both Championship and limited overs games, as well as fixtures against touring sides.

It would, of course, be impossible to produce a definitive list of the greatest ever matches, especially as nobody has ever watched the side in all of their games. An element of subjectivity is therefore needed, and this list has been drawn up based on the criteria of the context of the match and its wider importance in the history of the club.

Each Glamorgan supporter will have their own favourite match, beginning perhaps with the first time they saw the side in the flesh, or when they recorded one of the historic victories contained in this book.

If I were asked to choose my own personal favourite, I would have little hesitation in selecting the match at Sophia Gardens, Cardiff in 1976 when Glamorgan defeated Somerset by one run to deprive the West Country side of the Sunday League title. An odd choice you might say when I could opt for one of the Championship titles, a victory over a touring team or a visit to Lord's for a one-day final?

But for me, as a schoolboy in Cardiff, there was something extra that this victory over Somerset in 1976 symbolised. It was almost a throwback to the club's early days when defeat and strife were synonymous with the Welsh county. 1976 had been a poor summer for the club, and few people expected the downcast Glamorgan side to beat the talented Somerset team on that glorious Sunday in September. Out of a sense of loyalty, rather than expectation of a victory, I duly went down to the Cardiff ground and sat with my friends in the 'shed' at Sophia Gardens, surrounded by what seemed like the entire population of Somerset. Throughout the game we overheard and were subjected to various jibes and partisan comments against the Glamorgan side, so I can still vividly remember leaping in the air with my chums and (totally out of character!) cheering wildly when the visitors ended one run short of their target. How sweet the taste of success can be in the face of adversity!

Little did I think back in 1976 that, seventeen years later, I would be privileged to be in the dressing room at Canterbury after Glamorgan had beaten Kent to win the Sunday League title. My own, very personal, memory of that famous afternoon in September 1993 was to have the great Viv Richards crying tears of joy on my shoulder and for me to get a chance to thank the man who did so much for cricket in both Somerset and Glamorgan.

Neither could I have guessed back in 1976 that, twenty-one years later, I would be on Somerset soil itself toasting a Glamorgan success in the Championship. As at Canterbury in 1993, my memories of the classic match at Taunton in 1997 include the fine innings by Hugh Morris and Matthew Maynard, followed by the wonderful celebrations in the dressing room and on the balcony.

After all of the lows I had witnessed as an impressionable youngster since that day at Cardiff in 1976, these two classic matches at Canterbury and Taunton meant so much more. I hope that this book helps to stir similar memories, of victories achieved against the clock, dramatic wins over Test sides, stunning innings, fine bowling feats and wonderful catches.

Andrew Hignell
May 2001

Steve James, the captain of Glamorgan CCC in 2001 and the maker of the highest ever individual score in the county's history.

FOREWORD

I consider myself extremely fortunate to have played for Glamorgan during the 1990s and into the new Millennium, for it has arguably been the most successful period in the club's history. I have been part of a Championship-winning side, as well as a team that won the Sunday League and reached a Lord's final.

There have been many special moments, both for the team and for myself. On a personal level I was overjoyed, during the 2000 season, to overhaul Emrys Davies' sixty-one-year-old record of 287 (the highest ever individual score for Glamorgan) and go on to reach 309* at Colwyn Bay, a ground which has been so kind to me over the years.

However, when considering my greatest matches for Glamorgan, the ones which spring readily to mind are those when trophies have been lifted and celebrations begun. Canterbury in 1993 was my first taste of such an occasion and what a day it was! It was made all the more poignant by the fact that it was the great Sir Vivian Richards' last cricketing 'hurrah' and it was fitting that he should be there at the end, guiding us to victory.

It was the diminutive Tony Cottey, the heartbeat of our side until he surprisingly upped and left for Sussex at the end of 1998, who sneaked the winning runs with what he later recalled as 'a straight drive over the 'keeper's head'. I myself barely troubled the scorers that afternoon but it did not matter, for to be on the balcony on that late September evening was pure heaven.

Four years later we arrived at Taunton for the County Championship decider against Somerset. Again emotion was in the air as it turned out to be Hugh Morris' swansong at first-class level. Almost inevitably, he contributed a century and was supported by a quite sublime hundred from the skipper Matthew Maynard.

Fate dictated that we should need only 11 runs for victory in the second innings. A piece of cake you might think, but not for me entering *terra incognita*. I thought that maybe Somerset might be gentle and not bowl their usual bowlers, but I had not reckoned on the Whyte & Mackay rankings which that year were offering large sums of money for leading performers. Unfortunately, Andrew Caddick was near the top of the bowling rankings and hell bent on staying there – a couple of cheap Glamorgan wickets would see to that.

It has gone down in history that I scored the winning runs, but if the truth be known I made a complete 'horlicks' of the job. First of all, I was absolutely plumb LBW to Caddick – umpire George Sharp was in a charitable mood – then two balls later dropped at slip; a simple chance. The tension was getting to me and when I did eventually tickle Graham Rose to fine leg for four (Caddick had not moved across from the previous ball when Hugh Morris had got a single) I was not sure if we had won.

The crowds rushed on and I grabbed two stumps (my room-mate Adrian Dale had earlier pleaded with me to get him one) but I was not as quick-witted as Hugh and got caught in the mêlée. My bat (later returned after an appeal in the *South Wales Echo*) and one of the stumps were wrenched from me, and I trudged to the pavilion to give the bad news to Adrian. He was waiting at the bottom of the steps for me, with – would you believe it – two stumps in his hands! Hugh had given him one and his brother, who is a member of the Metropolitan Police, had wrestled the other from a spectator!

Great days, great memories and, fittingly, one of this book's classic matches. May there be many more of them.

Steve James, captain of Glamorgan CCC
May 2001

ACKNOWLEDGEMENTS

Once again, I am indebted to many people for helping me produce a book such as this. My thanks first of all to Steve James, the Glamorgan captain and beneficiary in 2001, for writing the enjoyable introduction, and to James Howarth for suggesting in the first place the idea for the book, and his subsequent advice and enthusiasm as it became a reality. I am also grateful to Mike Fatkin, the chief executive of Glamorgan, and Mrs Caryl Watkin for giving unlimited access to the club's scorebooks and photographic archives, from which many of the illustrations are drawn.

Many other people have helped to provide some of the other excellent photographs, including: Armine David; Simon, Georgina and Sara Turnbull; David Irving; Huw John; Bob Harragan; George Herringshaw of Associated Sports Photography; David Munden; David Smith; Mrs Elizabeth Parker-Jervis; Owain Howell; Peter Davies; Howard Evans and John Jenkins. Thanks also to the players of the Welsh county whose collective efforts over the years have produced these classic matches, to Kate Wiseman of Tempus for her help with the layout and to my wife Debra whose proof-reading skills once again were invaluable.

NB: Please note that on the scorecards ★ denotes the captain and + the wicketkeeper.

The Championship winning team of 1969. From left to right, back row: Eifion Jones, Bryan Davis, Malcolm Nash, Lawrence Williams, Roger Davis, Majid Khan. Front row: Tony Cordle, Peter Walker, Tony Lewis, Don Shepherd, Alan Jones.

21, 22 June	1889	*v.* **Warwickshire**	at Cardiff Arms Park	Friendly
22, 23 July	1897	*v.* **Cornwall**	at Swansea	Minor County Championship
1, 2, 3 Sept	1913	*v.* **Norfolk**	at Lakenham	Minor County Championship
18, 19, 20 May	1921	*v.* **Sussex**	at Cardiff Arms Park	County Championship
4, 6, 7 Aug	1923	*v.* **West Indians**	at Cardiff Arms Park	Tourist Match
31 Aug, 1, 2 Sept	1927	*v.* **Notts**	at Swansea	County Championship
15, 17, 18 June	1929	*v.* **Sussex**	at Horsham	County Championship
23, 25, 26 July	1932	*v.* **Somerset**	at Cowbridge	County Championship
24, 25, 26 Aug	1932	*v.* **Notts**	at Cardiff Arms Park	County Championship
1, 3 July	1935	*v.* **Northants**	at Llanelli	County Championship
8, 10, 11 July	1935	*v.* **South Africans**	at Cardiff Arms Park	Tourist Match
29, 30, 31 July	1936	*v.* **Worcestershire**	at Worcester	County Championship
19, 20, 21 May	1937	*v.* **Leicestershire**	at Leicester	County Championship
23, 24, 25 June	1937	*v.* **Worcestershire**	at Swansea	County Championship
31 July, 2, 3 Aug	1937	*v.* **N. Zealanders**	at Swansea	Tourist Match
24, 26, 27 May	1939	*v.* **West Indians**	at Cardiff Arms Park	Tourist Match
31 May, 1, 2 June	1939	*v.* **Gloucs**	at Newport	County Championship
16, 17, 18 June	1948	*v.* **Essex**	at Brentwood	County Championship
18, 19 Aug	1948	*v.* **Surrey**	at Cardiff Arms Park	County Championship
21, 23, 24 Aug	1948	*v.* **Hampshire**	at Bournemouth	County Championship
2, 4, 5 June	1951	*v.* **Derbyshire**	at Cardiff Arms Park	County Championship
4, 6 Aug	1951	*v.* **South Africans**	at Swansea	Tourist Match
10, 11, 12 May	1952	*v.* **Middlesex**	at Lord's	County Championship
6, 7, 8 July	1955	*v.* **Yorkshire**	at Harrogate	County Championship
16, 18, 19 May	1959	*v.* **Indians**	at Cardiff Arms Park	Tourist Match
22 May	1963	*v.* **Somerset**	at Cardiff Arms Park	Gillette Cup
1, 3, 4 Aug	1964	*v.* **Australians**	at Swansea	Tourist Match
9, 10 June	1965	*v.* **Yorkshire**	at Swansea	County Championship
28, 29, 30 July	1965	*v.* **Leicestershire**	at Ebbw Vale	County Championship
3, 4, 5 Aug	1968	*v.* **Australians**	at Swansea	Tourist Match
30 Aug, 1, 2 Sept	1969	*v.* **Essex**	at Swansea	County Championship
3, 4, 5 Sept	1969	*v.* **Worcestershire**	at Sophia Gardens	County Championship
5 Sept	1976	*v.* **Somerset**	at Sophia Gardens	Sunday League
17, 18, 19 Aug	1977	*v.* **Leicestershire**	at Swansea	Gillette Cup
3 Sept	1977	*v.* **Middlesex**	at Lord's	Gillette Cup
23 July	1978	*v.* **Sussex**	at Hastings	Sunday League
29, 31 Aug, 1 Sept	1981	*v.* **Essex**	at Colchester	County Championship
28, 29, 30 Aug	1985	*v.* **Notts**	at Trent Bridge	County Championship
16, 18, 19 June	1990	*v.* **Hampshire**	at Southampton	County Championship
21, 22, 23 July	1990	*v.* **Worcestershire**	at Abergavenny	County Championship
20, 21, 22 May	1992	*v.* **Warwickshire**	at Swansea	County Championship
1, 2, 3, 5 July	1993	*v.* **Middlesex**	at Sophia Gardens	County Championship
22, 23, 24, 25 July	1993	*v.* **Worcestershire**	at Worcester	County Championship
19 Sept	1993	*v.* **Kent**	at Canterbury	Sunday League
9 July	1997	*v.* **Hampshire**	at Southampton	NatWest Trophy
12, 13 Aug	1997	*v.* **Essex**	at Chelmsford	NatWest Trophy
18, 19, 20 Sept	1997	*v.* **Somerset**	at Taunton	County Championship
27, 28 May	2000	*v.* **Surrey**	at Sophia Gardens	Benson & Hedges Cup
10 June	2000	*v.* **Gloucs**	at Lord's	Benson & Hedges Cup
22, 23, 24, 25 Aug	2000	*v.* **Sussex**	at Colwyn Bay	County Championship

WARWICKSHIRE

21, 22 June 1889 at Cardiff Arms Park

Glamorgan's first ever competitive inter-county match ended in a resounding defeat for the Welsh club, who had been formed the previous year. During the winter of 1888/89 the county's eager officials had drawn up a fixture list and it included this inaugural contest against Warwickshire at the Arms Park in Cardiff.

Sadly, three of Glamorgan's key players were injured in the weeks leading up to this game, and, to compound matters, Warwickshire fielded a strong side, led by Ludford Docker, who had toured Australia with Arthur Shrewsbury's team in 1887/88, Arthur Lilley, one of the country's finest wicketkeepers and John Shilton, an accomplished fast bowler.

Edmund David of St Fagan's CC captained the predominantly amateur Glamorgan XI and, after winning the toss, he opted to take first use of the Arms Park wicket. But it proved not to be a fairytale start as off the second delivery Lewis Jenkins was dismissed and, despite some firm blows from Billy Bancroft and Theo Robinson, the vastly experienced Warwickshire bowlers dominated proceedings in the pre-lunch session.

With the scoreboard reading 81-9, it looked as if the Welsh county would make a rather embarrassing start, but their faces were saved by a rather jaunty last wicket partnership between Astley Samuel, an estate agent from Pontardawe, and Dan Thissen, the wicketkeeper from Morriston. They started to prosper against the tiring bowlers, and also confused the Warwickshire fielders by calling to each other in Welsh!

This gallant partnership took the score to 136, and it had lifted their morale as David led his team onto the field. James Lindley, the Cardiff professional, immediately struck by removing Docker, and he picked up a further four victims as the visitors found batting difficult against the accurate Glamorgan attack and lively fielding. Thissen also impressed behind the stumps with two catches and a smart stumping, as Warwickshire were restricted to a first innings lead of just two runs.

However, the Glamorgan batsmen failed to consolidate when they batted for a second time. Shilton took seven wickets, and only Gowan Clarke, a railway engineer from Cardiff CC, offered any resistance. It left the English county needing just 79 to win, which they comfortably reached in mid-afternoon for the loss of just two wickets. A large crowd had assembled in the hope of seeing another spirited fightback by the Glamorgan side, so with a couple of hours remaining, Warwickshire continued batting for exhibition purposes, to entertain the keen spectators.

Lewis Jenkins – the first Glamorgan player to be dismissed in a county game.

Edmund David, the captain of Glamorgan in their inaugural match in 1889.

Glamorgan won the toss and elected to bat Umpires: Not known

GLAMORGAN

			1ST INNINGS			2ND INNINGS	
L. Jenkins	c Richards	b Shilton	0	c Lilley	b Whitehead	7
D.E. Jones	c Lilley	b Bird	12	st Lilley	b Whitehead	12
A.W. Morris	c Bird	b Leake	9		b Shilton	8
W.J. Bancroft		b Shilton	13	c Leake	b Whitehead	1
T. Robinson	c Leake	b Shilton	19	lbw	b Shilton	15
*E.U. David	c Lilley	b Bird	0		b Shilton	2
J.G. Clarke	c D. Docker	b Bird	2		b Shilton	20
J.V. Lindley	lbw	b Shilton	7		b Shilton	3
W.E. Lewis	st Lilley	b Shilton	10	not out		9
A.W. Samuel	not out		28	c Richards	b Shilton	1
+D.E. Thissen	c Leake	b Whitehead	33	lbw	b Shilton	0
Extras			3			2
TOTAL			**136**			**80**

FOW: 1-0, 2-11, 3-37, 4-52, 5-52, 6-54, 7-60, 8-66, 9-81

1-1, 2-2, 3-11, 4-37, 5-39, 6-42, 7-42, 8-53, 9-74

Bowling	O	M	R	W		O	M	R	W
Shilton	36	16	49	5	Shilton	28.4	13	42	7
Leake	17	2	38	1	Bird	7	5	4	0
Bird	29	11	44	3	Whitehead	21	9	32	3
Whitehead	1.1	0	2	1					

WARWICKSHIRE

			1ST INNINGS			2ND INNINGS	
D. Docker	c David	b Lindley	8		b Samuel	0
A. Law		b Lindley	24	not out		26
W. Richards	st Thissen	b Samuel	0	lbw	b Robinson	21
*L.C. Docker	c Thissen	b Lindley	41	not out		25
C.F. Hunt		b Samuel	11			
W.F. Collishaw	retired hurt		0			
J.E. Shilton	c Bancroft	b Lindley	18			
A. Bird	c Thissen	b Lindley	1			
+A.F.A. Lilley	run out		8			
J. Leake	not out		8			
S.J. Whitehead		b Samuel	3			
Extras			16			7
TOTAL			**138**	(for 2 wickets)		**79**

FOW: 1-11, 2-16, 3-52, 4-88, 5-108, 6-110, 7-121, 8-133, 9-138

1-0, 2-35

Bowling	O	M	R	W		O	M	R	W
Lindley	26	7	51	5	Lindley	13	6	17	0
Samuel	21	7	56	3	Samuel	10.3	1	37	1
Robinson	6	1	15	0	Robinson	7	0	18	1

Glamorgan won by 8 wickets

CORNWALL

22, 23 July 1897 at Swansea

This was Glamorgan's first-ever win as a Minor County, having joined the second-class competition in 1897. The game also saw two other records being created – in their second innings, Cornwall were dismissed for 25, which is still the lowest total ever made in any match against Glamorgan, whilst in Cornwall's first innings, Sam Lowe, the Cardiff professional, took the first hat-trick recorded by a Glamorgan bowler.

Lowe was a thirty-year-old seam bowler who had played once for his native Nottinghamshire, in 1894. He subsequently joined Cardiff CC and acted as groundsman-professional at the Arms Park until 1906. His younger brother, Richard, followed him to South Wales and was also in the Glamorgan side for this match with Cornwall. He too had first-class experience with Nottinghamshire and Sussex, and together with his brother held a regular place in the Glamorgan side until the early 1900s.

Sam Lowe could be quite a hostile bowler, even on the slow St Helen's wicket, and his hat-trick against Cornwall was described as follows by the *South Wales Daily News* – 'Hosking, who had laboured for twenty minutes for just one was caught in the slips off Lowe, who had had downright bad luck to date. But with his next ball, the Cardiff bowler knocked over the middle stump of Colville-Smith, the Cornwall captain, and with his next, he bowled Trevarthen, so performing the hat-trick and gaining unreserved applause from the small band of spectators who had gathered at the St Helen's ground.'

Glamorgan had batted disappointingly in their first innings, but Lowe's efforts helped them to an 11-run lead. They fared much better in their second innings with Billy Bancroft and Bertie Letcher each making attractive fifties during a century partnership for the second wicket. Both eventually fell to Jesse Hide, who finished the match with fourteen victims.

As a result of Hide's excellent bowling, Cornwall were left a target of 259 in the three hours and twenty minutes that remained. It seemed a reasonable target, but they collapsed in dramatic fashion within the space of just three-quarters of an hour, and were bowled out for a paltry 25. Sam Lowe and William Lambert both took five wickets and, along with the rest of Joseph Brain's side, they were given a standing ovation as they left the field by the home crowd, few of whom could quite believe how easily and quickly Glamorgan had achieved their first win in the Minor County Championship.

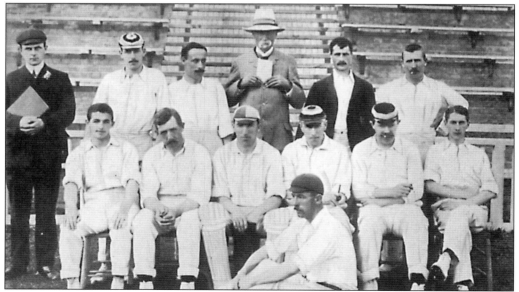

The Glamorgan team that dismissed Cornwall for 25. Sam Lowe is the player in the blazer in the back row.

GLAMORGAN

1ST INNINGS				2ND INNINGS			
E.W. Jones	c Blight	b Hide	6		b Hide	17	
W.J. Bancroft		b Hide	9	c Trevarthen	b Hide	71	
H.B. Letcher		b Hide	10	c Hosking	b Hide	57	
*J.H. Brain	c Colville-Smith	b Hide	48	c Coade	b Hide	16	
H.E. Morgan	c Coade	b Hosking	0	c Trevarthen	b Hide	0	
E.U. David		b Hide	6		b Hosking	4	
+W.H. Brain	lbw	b Hide	5	c Hosking	b Hide	12	
R. Lowe	not out		30	c Colville-Smith	b Hide	44	
W.S.R. Sweet-Escott		b Trevarthen	7	c Trevarthen	b Hide	4	
S. Lowe	c Tyack	b Trevarthen	0	not out		4	
W. Lambert	c Treweeke	b Trevarthen	0		b Hosking	1	
Extras			5			17	
TOTAL			**126**			**247**	

FOW: 1-13, 2-22, 3-39, 4-40, 5-61
6-79, 7-85, 8-126, 9-126   Not Known

Bowling	O	M	R	W		O	M	R	W
Hosking	16	4	50	1	Hosking	24.1	5	80	2
Hide	24	8	51	6	Hide	33	12	98	8
Blight	5	2	9	0	Blight	6	0	29	0
Trevarthen	3.2	0	11	3	Trevarthen	7	1	15	0
					Oates	4	2	8	0

CORNWALL

1ST INNINGS				2ND INNINGS			
Tyack		b Lambert	21		b Lambert	0	
+W. Coade	c and	b Lambert	39	st W. Brain	b Lambert	0	
W.H. Treweeke	st W. Brain	b Lambert	19		b S. Lowe	3	
Hosking	c Morgan	b S. Lowe	1		b S. Lowe	0	
J.B. Hide	c R. Lowe	b Lambert	4	c David	b Lambert	4	
Rev.W. Pickford		b Lambert	7	c Morgan	b S. Lowe	2	
*E. Colville-Smith		b S. Lowe	0	not out		0	
Trevarthen		b S. Lowe	0		b S. Lowe	3	
W.E. Oates		b Lambert	1	c W. Brain	b Lambert	6	
Blight	not out		5		b S. Lowe	1	
R.T. Mitchell		b S. Lowe	1		b Lambert	6	
Extras			17				
TOTAL			**115**			**25**	

FOW: 1-51, 2-84, 3-85, 4-89, 5-97   1-0, 2-0, 3-3, 4-3, 5-8,
6-97, 7-97, 8-97, 9-102   6-9, 7-16, 8-18, 9-18

Bowling	O	M	R	W		O	M	R	W
S. Lowe	18.3	10	27	4	S. Lowe	6	2	9	5
R. Lowe	9	1	21	0	Lambert	6.1	2	16	5
J.H. Brain	7	2	21	0					
Lambert	16	6	29	6					

Glamorgan won by 233 runs

NORFOLK

Glamorgan tasted further success as a Minor County, sharing the title in 1900 and, as the Minor County Championship changed into a knock-out format, reaching the final of the competition in 1907, 1908 and 1909. They lost each of these to Lancashire Second XI, Staffordshire and Wiltshire, and in 1913 they reached the final once again, eager to put aside their previous disappointments and to become the outright champions for the first ever time.

The 1913 final saw Glamorgan travel to Lakenham to play Norfolk in a game spanning three days in early September. Norfolk batted first, but only Reg Popham was at ease against the accurate Glamorgan seam attack, led by left-armer Harry Creber and right-armer Stamford Hacker. Each took four wickets and were supported by some deft wicketkeeping from Edgar Billings of Swansea CC, plus two fine catches from Billy Bancroft, the Welsh rugby international.

Glamorgan made a good start in reply, with captain Norman Riches and Jock Tait sharing a half-century stand, before Roderick Falconer dismissed the Glamorgan captain. His departure led to a swift change in fortunes, as wickets fell at regular intervals, and despite some hefty blows by Billings, Norfolk secured a first innings lead of 36 by the end of play on the second day.

Heavy overnight rain delayed the start on the final day, and when play resumed in the afternoon, the drying wicket was fully exploited by Harry Creber. The experienced bowler reverted to cut and spin, and he proved to be almost unplayable on the damp surface. Billings claimed two further stumpings, and when the last wicket fell, Norfolk were just 97 runs ahead.

By late afternoon, the wicket had eased, and as Norman Riches led his team off, they must have thought they had a reasonable chance of winning outright their first Minor County title. But the clouds had gathered again, and, as Riches and Tait strapped on their pads, rain started to fall. It gradually got worse, preventing any more play, so the outcome of the title was decided by the first innings totals. Norfolk were therefore adjudged champions, and the Glamorgan team made their long return journey by train, ruing their luck with the weather!

Harry Creber.

Billy Bancroft

NORFOLK

	1ST INNINGS			2ND INNINGS		
R.W. Thurgar		b Creber	12	c Bancroft	b Creber	6
R.F. Popham		b Hacker	74	c Maxwell	b Creber	12
G.A. Stephens	c Bancroft	b Maxwell	38	st Billings	b Creber	10
B. Cozens-Hardy	lbw	b Creber	14	c Hacker	b Creber	19
E.J. Fulcher		b Creber	35	run out		0
G.R. Pedden	c Riches	b Hacker	17		b Creber	1
A.R. Hudson	run out		1	c Tait	b Creber	3
Watson	c Billings	b Hacker	31	c Hacker	b Creber	4
J.H. Falcon	c Billings	b Hacker	0		b Hacker	0
Falconer	not out		7	st Billings	b Creber	5
Gibson	c Bancroft	b Creber	1	not out		1
Extras			14			
TOTAL			**244**			**61**

FOW: Not Known

Bowling	O	M	R	W		O	M	R	W
Creber	20.4	2	79	4	Creber	12.4	1	33	8
Hacker	32	8	79	4	Hacker	12	3	28	1
Maxwell	18	3	72	1					

GLAMORGAN 1ST INNINGS

*N.V.H. Riches	c Fulcher	b Falconer	38
J.R. Tait	c Watson	b Fulcher	46
R.A. Gibbs	c Pedden	b Fulcher	0
T.A.L. Whittington	lbw	b Fulcher	18
E.R. Sweet-Escott	c Watson	b Fulcher	4
W.J. Bancroft	c Cozens-Hardy	b Falconer	12
W.P. Morris		b Falconer	11
J. Maxwell	c Stephens	b Falconer	0
+E.A. Billings		b Fulcher	21
W.S. Hacker	not out		0
H. Creber	lbw	b Falconer	0
Extras			18
TOTAL			**168**

FOW: Not Known

Bowling	O	M	R	W
Falconer	31.3	15	49	5
Fulcher	22	9	26	5
Gibson	11	5	18	0
Watson	27	10	41	0
Falcon	3	0	13	0
Hudson	3	1	3	0

Norfolk won on first innings

Sussex

18, 19, 20 May 1921 at Cardiff Arms Park

Glamorgan's bid to secure first-class status achieved success during the autumn of 1920 as the MCC admitted the Welsh county into the County Championship for 1921. During the winter months, the county's playing resources were strengthened by the agreement of bowlers Stamford Hacker, Jack Nash, Harry Creber and former Yorkshire batsman William Bates to play as the club's professionals, and all for the princely sum of £14 for each away match, and £10 for home games.

The club's modest finances, however, meant that no more professionals could be hired, so when captain Norman Riches and his team gathered for their inaugural first-class fixture against Sussex on 18 May 1921, he had at his disposal a mainly amateur side. In contrast, Sussex were at full strength, and their team included such notable players as bowler Maurice Tate, batsmen Ted Bowley, England all-rounder Vallance Jupp and the Gilligan brothers – Arthur and Alfred.

Riches struck the first blow by winning the toss and, in front of a crowd in excess of 5,000, bathed in glorious sunshine, he opened the batting with Tom Whittington. All of the Glamorgan

Norman Riches (extreme right) leads the team onto the field at the Arms Park in 1921 for Glamorgan's first County Championship fixture.

Jock Tait – the man who almost became Glamorgan's first Championship centurion.

batsmen proceeded to make useful contributions against the accurate Sussex attack, but it was their number eight batsman Henry Symonds who ended up as top scorer. The thirty-one-year-old left-hander from Cardiff CC made an assured half-century and, together with club colleague George Cording, a Cardiff schoolmaster, they shared an attractive seventh-wicket partnership of 76.

Glamorgan were eventually dismissed for 272 and, buoyed by the success of their batsmen, the Welsh bowlers soon made early inroads into the Sussex batting. Veteran off-cutter Jack Nash picked up four cheap wickets, whilst Edgar Cooper, a thirty-year-old fast medium seamer from Briton Ferry CC, also claimed four victims as Sussex were dismissed for 152.

The crowd gather in front of the Arms Pavilion after their famous victory over Sussex in 1921.

It was then the turn of Glamorgan's batsmen to struggle against the Sussex bowlers – all that is except Jock Tait, the thirty-four-year-old amateur from Cardiff CC. Tait had been born in the Shetland Islands, and he had already enjoyed quite a distinguished sporting career, winning a Welsh amateur football cap in 1913, as well as playing rugby for Swansea. Despite the loss of partners at regular intervals, Tait unfurled some bold and uninhibited strokes, and, by the close of play on the second day, he was unbeaten on 96 and poised to become Glamorgan's first-ever centurion in Championship cricket.

When play resumed on the final morning, Maurice Tate sportingly bowled his namesake a gentle full toss down the leg side, hoping that Tait would reach three figures and record this milestone in Welsh sport. But nerves had taken over – Tait swung and missed, and he was then clean bowled by Tate's next delivery, and dejectedly trudged off the Arms Park arena, knowing that he had come within a whisker of making history.

By the time the last Glamorgan wicket fell, Sussex were left with a rather stiff target of 334. Their position soon became even worse, as they slumped to 59-3 as Cooper and Creber once again made early inroads. Ted Bowley and Felix Jenner then halted the decline with a spirited stand of 166 for the fourth wicket, and their efforts gave the visitors a realistic chance of pulling off a fine victory.

For once, Nash proved ineffective on the Cardiff wicket, and with the Sussex total mounting, Riches was forced to recall Cooper in a desperate bid to break the troublesome stand. It proved a wise decision as firstly Jenner was caught by Symonds, before Cooper picked up two further wickets to tip the balance slightly back in Glamorgan's favour. A revitalised Nash then returned to take the wicket of Bowley, and the crowd started to sense that a Glamorgan victory might occur.

Alfred Gilligan offered some stubborn resistance, but Creber returned to mop up the tail. When last man Henry Roberts was caught by Percy Morris, Sussex were 24 runs short of their target, and many of the crowd ran onto the field to congratulate Riches and his team. The two teams then gathered on the pavilion balcony, and both captain's made impromptu speeches. Riches began by paying tribute to Tom Whittington, the club's secretary who had secured both the finances and fixtures needed for entry into the Championship. Arthur Gilligan then graciously congratulated the Welsh side, saying how they 'had given us a magnificent game, and we do not mind being beaten in the slightest. We have been down until today, but today we might have won. We did not – Glamorgan did, and I congratulate them very much.'

GLAMORGAN

	1ST INNINGS			2ND INNINGS	
T.A.L. Whittington	c Street	b A.E. Gilligan	40	c A.E. Gilligan b Cox	27
*N.V.H. Riches	c A.H. Gilligan	b Jupp	16	b Tate	3
W.E. Bates		b A.E. Gilligan	39	lbw b Cox	8
W.P. Morris		b Tate	7	b A.H. Gilligan	13
J.R. Tait		b Cox	31	b Tate	96
+G.E. Cording	c Cox	b Roberts	45	c A.H. Gilligan b Roberts	10
A. O'Bree		b Cox	0	b A.H. Gilligan	8
H.G. Symonds	c Higgs	b Bowley	58	b Cox	20
E. Cooper		b Jupp	12	b Cox	0
H. Creber	not out		7	b Cox	7
A. Nash		b Cox	5	not out	5
Extras		(B 5, LB 5, W 1, NB 1)	12	(B 13, LB 3)	16
TOTAL			**272**		**213**

FOW: 1-38, 2-78, 3-99, 4-115, 5-169,   1-25, 2-41, 3-52, 4-107, 5-120,
6-169, 7-245, 8-252, 9-262   6-137, 7-171, 8-171, 9-197

Bowling	O	M	R	W	Bowling	O	M	R	W
Roberts	15	2	31	1	Roberts	9	0	21	1
Tate	26	12	34	1	Tate	13.2	4	29	2
Jupp	21	5	52	2	Jupp	15	4	37	0
Cox	20.5	5	36	3	Cox	23	4	60	5
A.H. Gilligan	5	0	24	0	A.H. Gilligan	7	0	33	2
A.E. Gilligan	21	3	71	2	A.E. Gilligan	6	2	17	0
Bowley	5	1	12	1					

SUSSEX

	1ST INNINGS			2ND INNINGS	
V.W.C. Jupp	c Cording	b Cooper	34	c O'Bree b Cooper	5
E.H. Bowley	lbw	b Nash	21	b Nash	146
K.A. Higgs		b Nash	0	lbw b Creber	5
M.W. Tate		b Cooper	11	c Nash b Creber	10
F.D. Jenner		b Nash	6	c Symonds b Cooper	55
+G. Street	c Bates	b Cooper	5	(9) b Nash	11
*A.E.R. Gilligan		b Cooper	3	(6) c and b Cooper	15
G. Stannard	c Tait	b Nash	41	(7) c Riches b Cooper	4
G.R. Cox	not out		7	(10) not out	11
A.H.H. Gilligan	run out		2	(8) c Tait b Creber	33
H.E. Roberts	c Cording	b Creber	13	c Morris b Creber	0
Extras		(LB 7, W 1, NB 1)	9	(B 8, LB 6, W 1)	15
TOTAL			**152**		**310**

FOW: 1-44, 2-48, 3-65, 4-78, 5-80,   1-11, 2-45, 3-59, 4-225, 5-249,
6-83, 7-103, 8-131, 9-134   6-251, 7-258, 8-289, 9-303

Bowling	O	M	R	W	Bowling	O	M	R	W
Creber	17.5	6	25	1	Creber	19.2	1	78	4
Morris	4	1	12	0	Morris	3	0	20	0
Nash	29	11	45	4	Nash	25	1	86	2
Cooper	16	2	61	4	Cooper	24	3	81	4
					Bates	6	0	29	0
					Symonds	1	0	1	0

Glamorgan won by 23 runs

THE WEST INDIANS

4, 6, 7 August 1923 at Cardiff Arms Park

By the time Glamorgan played the West Indian touring team in August 1923, the club had suffered a series of heavy defeats in the County Championship. In all, they had lost 45 of their 61 fixtures, including 18 of them by an innings. Morale in the dressing room had slumped, and various key players from previous years had retired. Although a few new faces had been hired or given trials, the side were still struggling and few people gave the Glamorgan side much of a chance against the tourists.

Their pessimism appeared well-founded as Glamorgan mustered just 115 in their first innings and the Caribbean side were able to secure a first innings lead of 86. It might have been more had it not been for the efforts of Trevor Arnott, the cheerful amateur, who opened the Welsh attack. He refused to be downhearted, and took 7-40 as the West Indians were bowled out for 201.

Arnott's efforts with the ball roused the Glamorgan batsmen, who gave a better account of themselves in their second innings. William Bates drew on his vast experience to carefully see off the new ball, before Jimmy Stone, the former Hampshire wicketkeeper, and Frank Pinch, the Cornish-born schoolmaster, shared an attractive partnership of 136 in just 90 minutes. Despite the loss of Pinch for 55, Stone continued to counter-attack and, with useful support from Arnott, the forty-six-year-old veteran became the club's first centurion against a touring team.

Stone's brave efforts boosted morale in the Glamorgan camp as the West Indians prepared to make 239 to win the game. However, the batting of George Challenor soon dampened the Welsh enthusiasm. Despite the loss of a few partners, Challenor played almost without fault, and with the score on 185-5, it looked as if he was going to play a match-winning innings for the tourists.

Soon after reaching a fine century, however, Jack Mercer was brought back into the attack, and the former Sussex seam bowler trapped Challenor leg before. Spinner Frank Ryan then claimed two quick wickets at the other end, and the large Cardiff crowd suddenly sensed a historic victory. Mercer did not disappoint them, claiming the last two wickets, before great celebrations began in honour of Glamorgan's first ever triumph over a touring team.

The West Indian players take to the field at the Arms Park.

GLAMORGAN

Batsman	1ST INNINGS	R	2ND INNINGS	R
*N.V.H. Riches lbw	b John	5	b John	26
T.R. Morgan	b Browne	29	c Dewhurst b Pascall	12
W.E. Bates	b John	20	c Challenor b John	51
C.F. Walters	b Browne	0	b John	0
J. Stone c Austin	b John	19	c and b Constantine	108
F.B. Pinch	b John	4	b Francis	55
D. Davies	b John	0	b Pascall	10
T. Arnott not out		15	st Dewhurst b Pascall	32
F.P. Ryan	b John	1	b Francis	7
J. Mercer	b John	9	not out	4
+D. Sullivan run out		1	c Tarilton b Francis	0
Extras	(B 2, LB 10)	12	(B 14, LB 4, NB 1)	19
TOTAL		**115**		**324**

FOW: 1-13, 2-39, 3-46, 4-81, 5-85, 6-87, 7-97, 8-102, 9-114

FOW (2nd): 1-22, 2-53, 3-53, 4-128, 5-265, 6-267, 7-298, 8-319, 9-324

Bowling	O	M	R	W		O	M	R	W
John	23	9	52	7	John	31	5	95	3
Francis	8	2	23	0	Francis	30.3	6	77	3
Browne	14	5	28	2	Browne	11	4	36	0
					Pascall	15	4	37	3
					Small	6	1	28	0
					Constantine	6	0	32	1

WEST INDIANS

Batsman	1ST INNINGS	R	2ND INNINGS	R
G. Challenor	b Arnott	5	lbw b Mercer	110
P.H. Tarilton c Sullivan	b Arnott	75	b Pinch	9
H.W. Ince	b Pinch	21	lbw b Ryan	25
*H.B.G. Austin lbw	b Ryan	40 (5)	c Sullivan b Mercer	24
J.A. Small c Pinch	b Arnott	4 (4)	c and b Arnott	0
C.R. Browne c Sullivan	b Arnott	0	st Sullivan b Ryan	4
V.S. Pascall	b Arnott	6	c and b Ryan	0
L.N. Constantine not out		9	c Sullivan b Mercer	3
+G.A.R. Dewhurst	b Arnott	3	c D. Davies b Mercer	0
G.N. Francis st Sullivan	b Mercer	12	run out	2
G. John	b Arnott	5	not out	2
Extras	(B 15, LB 6)	21	(B 12, LB 4)	16
TOTAL		**201**		**195**

FOW: 1-14, 2-83, 3-159, 4-161, 5-162, 6-163, 7-180, 8-184, 9-190

FOW (2nd): 1-21, 2-100, 3-101, 4-171, 5-184, 6-185, 7-189, 8-190, 9-193

Bowling	O	M	R	W	Bowling	O	M	R	W
Mercer	24	3	65	1	Mercer	12	1	41	4
Arnott	14.2	2	40	7	Arnott	12	0	49	1
Ryan	9	1	20	1	Ryan	14.2	0	71	3
D. Davies	7	0	15	0	D. Davies	3	0	10	0
Pinch	5	1	22	1	Pinch	3	1	8	1
Bates	4	0	18	0					

Glamorgan won by 43 runs

NOTTINGHAMSHIRE

31 August, 1, 2 September 1927 at Swansea

Glamorgan had had a relatively disastrous 1927 season – they had not won any of their 25 Championship matches, and travelled to Swansea for the final game of the season to play Nottinghamshire who seemed poised to clinch the county title. In fact, all that Nottinghamshire needed to become champions was a draw, so with Glamorgan having such a dreadful season, plans had already been set in motion in Nottingham for a civic reception to celebrate their title-winning season.

But Glamorgan upset their plans, winning this game against everyone's expectations and apart from a short time on the first day, the Welsh side were in complete control. By mid-afternoon on the first day, Frank Ryan, the idiosyncratic spinner, had claimed five wickets as Nottinghamshire were dismissed for 233. The game was then transformed, initially by a partnership of 158 for the first wicket by William Bates and John Bell, with each of the Glamorgan openers dominating the Nottinghamshire attack.

Bell was eventually trapped for 57, and although four of his colleagues soon followed him back to the St Helen's pavilion, Bates remained undeterred. He received stoic support from Arnold Dyson, Joe Hills and wicketkeeper Dennis Sullivan, and by the time Bates was eventually dismissed, Glamorgan had reached a quite impressive 375, with a useful lead on first innings of 142.

With only a day to go, and the Swansea wicket appearing to be quite benign, the Nottinghamshire batsmen knew that all was required to become county champions was to occupy the crease for the rest of the game. Given the modest form of the Glamorgan bowlers it seemed a formality, but Jack Mercer and Frank Ryan had other ideas – Mercer quickly took the first three wickets in a fine new ball spell that reduced Nottinghamshire to 30 for 3, and sent the alarm bells ringing in their camp. Ryan then got into the action as he tricked and teased the visiting batsmen with his subtle spin.

Every false stroke brought a wicket, as the Nottinghamshire players returned to the pavilion almost shell-shocked, realising that their dream was rapidly turning into a nightmare. Indeed, there are tales of one of the Nottinghamshire tailenders sitting on the pavilion steps with tears flooding down his cheeks as his team-mates came back to the dressing rooms at regular intervals. His side were finally dismissed for 61 as Glamorgan secured a rare innings victory, and the county title ultimately went to Lancashire.

Payton is bowled by Mercer during Nottinghamshire's dramatic collapse at Swansea.

NOTTINGHAMSHIRE

		1ST INNINGS			2ND INNINGS	
G. Gunn		b Arnott	68	c Arnott	b Mercer	2
W.W. Whysall	run out		16	c Arnott	b Mercer	10
W. Walker	c and	b D. Davies	11		b Mercer	0
W.R.D. Payton	c Sullivan	b Ryan	50		b Mercer	10
+B. Lilley	not out		44 (6)	c Arnott	b Ryan	1
W.A. Flint	c Hills	b Ryan	3 (5)		b Mercer	7
S.J. Staples	lbw	b Arnott	26	lbw	b Ryan	0
*L. Kirk		b Ryan	1		b Mercer	0
F. Barratt	c Arnott	b Ryan	0		b Ryan	11
T.L. Richmond		b Mercer	1	c Mercer	b Ryan	1
W. Voce	st Sullivan	b Ryan	0	not out		7
Extras		(B 8, LB 1, NB 4)	13		(B 6, LB 4, W 1, NB 1)	12
TOTAL			**233**			**61**

FOW: 1-29, 2-45, 3-143, 4-165, 5-178,   1-12, 2-14, 3-30, 4-33, 5-34,
          6-196, 7-198, 8-226, 9-232   6-36, 7-42, 8-43, 9-44

Bowling	O	M	R	W	Bowling	O	M	R	W
Mercer	30	9	51	1	Mercer	14	3	31	6
Arnott	12	2	45	2	Arnott	2	1	4	0
Ryan	30.2	5	81	5	Ryan	11.2	4	14	4
D. Davies	11	4	22	1					
Bates	6	0	21	0					

GLAMORGAN   1ST INNINGS

W.E. Bates	lbw	b Richmond	163
J.T. Bell	lbw	b Staples	57
J.T. Morgan	st Lilley	b Richmond	0
*T. Arnott	c Barratt	b Richmond	1
D. Davies	c Voce	b Richmond	0
W.G. Morgan		b Barratt	7
A.H. Dyson	c Voce	b Richmond	27
J.J. Hills	c and	b Flint	39
+D. Sullivan		b Flint	31
J. Mercer		b Staples	1
F.P. Ryan	not out		8
Extras		(B 23, LB 17, W 1)	41
TOTAL			**375**

FOW: 1-158, 2-159, 3-169, 4-183, 5-226
          6-268, 7-295, 8-351, 9-352

Bowling	O	M	R	W
Barratt	14	3	45	1
Staples	55	24	104	2
Richmond	42	9	102	5
Voce	24	8	56	0
Flint	9	1	27	2

Glamorgan won by an innings and 81 runs

SUSSEX

15, 17, 18 June 1929 at Horsham

Only a handful of sides in Championship history have ever won after following-on, but in 1929 the Glamorgan side, under the captaincy of Trevor Arnott, achieved this feat at Horsham against Sussex. Surely few of those present on the first day of the game could have forecast the dramatic turnaround, especially as they had seen Sussex total 306 with Ted Bowley making a workmanlike 130. Then, when Glamorgan batted, they were soon in trouble against the bowling of Bert Wensley, and by the close of the first day's play were 57-5.

Sussex remained in control on the second morning, quickly taking the remaining five wickets and, shortly before lunch, the Glamorgan openers were back at the crease as the Welsh side followed on. Second time around, they offered a little more in the way of resistance, with John Bell making a stubborn half-century. Yet by the time that the arrears had been cleared off, Bell was one of five batsmen already back in the Horsham pavilion.

It seemed like only a matter of time before Sussex wrapped up the match, but Guy Morgan, the twenty-two-year-old Welsh rugby international, then turned the game on its head with what proved to be a remarkable match-winning innings. The Cambridge undergraduate had been in useful form with the bat earlier in the season for the University side, but the young all-rounder had been primarily drafted into the Glamorgan side in an attempt to improve the county's fielding.

Morgan proceeded to play the finest innings of his life, counter-attacking the tiring Sussex bowlers and, together with Trevor Arnott, they added 78 for the seventh wicket before Arnott was dismissed one short of an impressive half-century. Despite the loss of his captain, Morgan then took complete control, hitting boundaries all around the wicket, and marshalling the bowling to protect the tailenders. Frank Ryan also lent useful support, adding 85 for the final wicket, so by the time Ryan was dismissed Glamorgan had extended their lead to 203, with Morgan remaining unbeaten on 91.

Encouraged by this spirited fightback, the Glamorgan bowlers went back out, and reduced Sussex to 80-8. Jack Mercer and Emrys Davies proved almost unplayable, before Tommy Cook and Walter Cornford added an air of respectability to the Sussex innings. When Cornford was finally dismissed for 25, Glamorgan had won a truly remarkable contest, and it was fitting that Trevor Arnott should ask Guy Morgan to lead the victorious Glamorgan side off the field.

Far left: The jovial Trevor Arnott. Left: A cartoon caricature of Guy Morgan. As well as playing cricket for Glamorgan, he was also a Welsh rugby international.

SUSSEX

		1ST INNINGS			2ND INNINGS	
E.H. Bowley	lbw	b Bates	130		b Mercer	4
J.H. Parks	st Every	b Ryan	21		b Mercer	26
John Langridge	c Hills	b Bates	3		b D.E. Davies	6
T.E.R. Cook	c Bates	b D.E. Davies	43	not out		54
James Langridge	c Bell	b D.E. Davies	0	lbw	b Mercer	0
A.F. Wensley	st Every	b D.E. Davies	47	st Every	b D.E. Davies	4
A.H.H. Gilligan		b Arnott	22		b Mercer	4
G.A.K. Collins	c Hills	b Mercer	14	c Bates	b D.E. Davies	3
G.S. Pearce		b D.E. Davies	1	c Bell	b D.E. Davies	9
*A.E.R. Gilligan		b D.E. Davies	0		b Mercer	2
+W.L. Cornford	not out		4	lbw	b Bates	25
Extras		(B 5, LB 11, NB 5)	21		(B 1, LB 6, W 1, NB 2)	10
TOTAL			**306**			**147**

FOW: 1-34, 2-65, 3-208, 4-209, 5-222
6-267, 7-291, 8-294, 9-298

1-4, 2-40, 3-44, 4-44, 5-51
6-56, 7-63, 8-77, 9-80

Bowling	O	M	R	W	Bowling	O	M	R	W
Mercer	31.5	7	77	1	Mercer	23	1	77	5
Arnott	20	3	73	1	Arnott	4	2	6	0
Ryan	13	3	41	1	Ryan	6	0	14	0
Bates	12	0	65	2	Bates	1.5	0	6	1
D. Davies	2	0	3	0	D.E. Davies	20	8	34	4
D.E. Davies	14	4	26	5					

GLAMORGAN

		1ST INNINGS			2ND INNINGS	
W.E. Bates	lbw	b Wensley	16	c Wensley	b Jas Langridge	25
J.T. Bell		b Parks	1	c Parks	b Wensley	56
J.J. Hills	c Parks	b Jas Langridge	26	c John Langridge	b Bowley	29
*T. Arnott	c Cornford	b Jas Langridge	1	(7) c John Langridge	b Parks	49
D. Davies	c Bowley	b Wensley	1	(4) c Jas Langridge	b Bowley	13
F.W. Mathias		b Wensley	10	st Cornford	b Bowley	48
W.G. Morgan	lbw	b Wensley	8	(8) not out		91
D.E. Davies	not out		12	(5) c Parks	b Jas Langridge	33
J. Mercer	c John Langridge	b Jas Langridge	5	(10) run out		7
F.P. Ryan	c Jas Langridge	b Wensley	5	(11) st Cornford	b Cook	29
+T. Every	c Bowley	b Jas Langridge	7	(9) c Collins	b Bowley	2
Extras		(B 4, LB 5)	9		(B 18, LB 7, W 1)	26
TOTAL			**101**			**408**

FOW: 1-1, 2-31, 3-46, 4-47, 5-57,
6-72, 7-75, 8-80, 9-86

1-78, 2-100, 3-127, 4-137, 5-191,
6-224, 7-302, 8-314, 9-323

Bowling	O	M	R	W		O	M	R	W
Parks	10	4	18	1	Parks	26	10	56	1
Wensley	24	5	49	5	Wensley	42	15	87	1
Jas Langridge	14.3	4	25	4	Jas Langridge	42	11	86	2
					Bowley	42	11	115	4
					Pearce	2	0	10	0
					A.E.R. Gilligan	5	0	19	0
					Cook	2	0	9	1

Glamorgan won by 56 runs

SOMERSET

23, 25, 26 July 1932 at Cowbridge

There were fewer finer off-spinners in county cricket during the 1930s than Johnnie Clay. His clever spin and cunning change of length meant that he was a handful on the truest of wickets, so when it came to facing Clay on a damp, spiteful surface, the opposing batsmen were certainly on a sticky wicket!

This was the case at Cowbridge in 1932, where weekend rain had transformed the state of Glamorgan's Championship encounter with Somerset. On the Saturday afternoon, Maurice Turnbull had given a dazzling display of strokeplay, dancing down the wicket to drive the Somerset bowlers, time after time, back over their heads, and through the covers. In all, the Glamorgan captain hit 13 majestic boundaries in a stay at the crease of barely over an hour and a half, and by the time rain had started to fall in late afternoon, his side had reached 237-7.

No more play was possible until half past two on the Monday afternoon, by which time the rains had changed the nature of the Cowbridge wicket. Rather than declare immediately, Turnbull instructed his tail-enders to go for quick runs, knowing that a little bit more action would help to loosen the surface even more. Mercer responded with a quickfire 31 made in just 9 minutes, and his efforts saw the Welsh county to 281.

Somerset were soon in deep trouble, slumping to 31-6, as Clay immediately hit a perfect length and exploited the cracked and pot-marked surface. Arthur Wellard made a few lusty blows, but he fell to the gentle left-arm spin of Emrys Davies, as Clay took 5-28 and Turnbull invited Somerset to follow-on 193 runs behind.

It was not long before Clay was back in the wickets, dismissing Jack Lee and Michael Bennett as Somerset lurched to 5-2. Rain then interrupted proceedings yet again, with play being suspended until one o'clock on Tuesday afternoon. It then took a mere seventy minutes for Clay and Mercer to finish off the Somerset resistance. Clay only claimed a further two wickets, but his accuracy forced the Somerset batsmen to chance their arm at the other end against the seam of Mercer. The latter was rewarded with wonderful figures of 6-15, as Somerset were dismissed for 40, and all without any of their batsmen reaching double figures.

Johnnie Clay

Trevor Every, Glamorgan's wicketkeeper.

GLAMORGAN   1ST INNINGS

A.H. Dyson	c and	b White	6
D.E. Davies	c Burrough	b Young	41
C.C. Smart	c Luckes	b Young	21
D. Davies	c Wellard	b Lee	28
*M.J.L. Turnbull	c Lee	b Hazell	81
R.G. Duckfield		b White	10
+T. Every		b White	16
A.H. Howard	c Hazell	b White	10
J.C. Clay		b White	17
G. Lavis	not out		8
J. Mercer	c Wellard	b White	31
Extras		(B 8, LB 4)	12
TOTAL			**281**

FOW: 1-25, 2-64, 3-81, 4-176, 5-193,
         6-197, 7-225, 8-242, 9-249

Bowling	O	M	R	W
Andrews	8	3	20	0
Wellard	5	2	7	0
Lee	17	5	73	1
White	54.3	24	82	6
Hazell	34	14	52	1
Young	25	13	35	2

SOMERSET   1ST INNINGS   2ND INNINGS

J.W. Lee		b Clay	1	lbw	b Clay	0
A. Young		b Clay	10	c Turnbull	b Mercer	4
G.M. Bennett		b Clay	0		b Clay	1
*R.A. Ingle		b D.E. Davies	4	c Every	b Mercer	9
J.C. White		b Mercer	24		b Mercer	1
C.C. Case	lbw	b Clay	0		b Clay	1
H.D. Burrough	lbw	b D.E. Davies	0		b Mercer	4
A.W. Wellard	c Clay	b D.E. Davies	27		b Mercer	0
W.H.R. Andrews		b Mercer	9		b Clay	5
+W.T. Luckes	not out		6	not out		6
H.L. Hazell	c Duckfield	b Clay	0	c Turnbull	b Mercer	3
Extras		(B 6, LB 1)	7		(LB 3, NB 3)	6
TOTAL			**88**			**40**

FOW: 1-4, 2-4, 3-9, 4-30, 5-30,   1-4, 2-5, 3-12, 4-13, 5-20,
         6-31, 7-65, 8-82, 9-83   6-20, 7-20, 8-31, 9-33

Bowling	O	M	R	W	Bowling	O	M	R	W
Mercer	12	6	12	2	Mercer	9.3	4	15	6
Clay	22.1	7	28	5	Clay	9	2	19	4
D.E. Davies	17	6	41	3					

Glamorgan won by an innings and 153 runs

NOTTINGHAMSHIRE
24, 25, 26 August 1932 at Cardiff Arms Park

In August 1932 at the Arms Park, Harold Larwood and Bill Voce experimented with 'bodyline' bowling, prior to their winter tour with the MCC to Australia. It was the final Championship match of the season, and with the touring party having already been announced, the game with Glamorgan gave the Nottinghamshire opening pair a final chance to practise with fast leg-theory before travelling 'down under' for the Ashes series against Don Bradman and the other gifted Australian batsmen. Based on their efforts at the Arms Park, the experiment was a complete failure as Maurice Turnbull scored a quite superb double-hundred, and shared a fine partnership of 220 for the second wicket with Dai Davies, who in turn made a solid century.

This followed Nottinghamshire's first innings of 386, which had given their captain, Arthur Carr, what he thought would be enough runs on the board to try out 'bodyline' bowling, with its ring of leg side catchers. Short ball after short ball was delivered by Larwood and Voce, but Turnbull and Davies remained undeterred, and hit boundary after boundary.

Turnbull was by far the more aggressive of the two Glamorgan batsmen. Despite the barrage of short rising deliveries up towards his ribcage, the Glamorgan captain hooked, pulled and cut the ball with great power, sometimes putting the spectators at a greater risk of being hit than himself, as the ball sped to, and over, the boundary ropes time and again.

In all, Turnbull's magnificent double hundred contained 2 sixes and 24 fours, and hugely impressed the large contingent of cricket writers who had travelled to the Arms Park knowing of the intentions of the Nottinghamshire bowlers to practice the new theory of attack. As one journalist later wrote, 'if fast leg theory had been judged on what Turnbull and Davies did to it at Cardiff, there would have been no storms later on in Australia.'

In fact, Turnbull had the last laugh on the final afternoon as Nottinghamshire ended up battling to avoid defeat. Seam bowler Ted Glover took three wickets as the visitors slumped to 62-4, before a couple of chances were then spilled, allowing Willis Walker and Frank Shipston to save the day for the rather embarrassed Nottinghamshire side.

Cigarette card images depicting the two stars of this classic match – Maurice Turnbull (left) and Harold Larwood (right).

Nottinghamshire won the toss and elected to bat　　*Umpires: D. Hendren and F. Field*

NOTTINGHAMSHIRE

	1ST INNINGS				2ND INNINGS		
W.W. Keeton	c Duckfield	b Mercer	22			b Lavis	13
C.B. Harris		b D.E. Davies	12		c D.E. Davies	b Glover	20
W. Walker	run out		68			not out	67
*A.W. Carr	c D.E. Davies	b Glover	92 (7)		not out		17
A. Staples	c and	b Mercer	31		c Howard	b Glover	0
F.W. Shipston	not out		102		c D. Davies	b Glover	25
+B. Lilley		b D. Davies	15				
J. Hardstaff		b Mercer	7 (4)		c Howard	b Glover	1
H. Larwood		b D.E. Davies	16				
W. Voce		b D.E. Davies	14				
S.J. Staples		b Lavis	0				
Extras		(LB 3, NB 4)	7		(B 12, LB 3, W 1, NB 2)		18
TOTAL			**386**		(for 5 wickets)		**161**

FOW:　1-26, 2-42, 3-158, 4-216, 5-238
　　　6-276, 7-291, 8-327, 9-371

　　　1-17, 2-57, 3-61, 4-62, 5-123

Bowling	O	M	R	W	Bowling	O	M	R	W
Mercer	40	12	110	3	Mercer	10	0	24	0
Glover	20	2	97	1	Glover	18	1	52	4
Lavis	25.3	9	65	1	Lavis	9	3	12	1
D.E. Davies	29	2	75	3	D.E. Davies	22	6	40	0
D. Davies	9	2	32	1	Boon	2	0	12	0
					Turnbull	1	0	3	0

GLAMORGAN　　　1ST INNINGS

A.H. Dyson		b Larwood	36
D.E. Davies		b Voce	30
D. Davies	st Lilley	b S. Staples	106
*M.J.L. Turnbull	c Voce	b Larwood	205
R.G. Duckfield		b Larwood	5
+T. Every	not out		58
A.H. Howard	c and	b Larwood	0
R.W. Boon		b Larwood	0
G. Lavis	st Lilley	b Harris	22
J. Mercer	st Lilley	b S. Staples	9
E.R.K. Glover	c A. Staples	b S. Staples	2
Extras		(B 24, LB 4, NB 1)	29
TOTAL			**502**

FOW:　1-53, 2-96, 3-316, 4-354, 5-436
　　　6-438, 7-438, 8-477, 9-492

Bowling	O	M	R	W
Larwood	30	2	78	5
Voce	27	4	96	1
S. Staples	48	10	117	3
A. Staples	34	7	89	0
Harris	14	1	64	1
Hardstaff	9	0	29	0

Match Drawn

NORTHAMPTONSHIRE

1, 3 July 1935 at Llanelli

Glamorgan's visit to Stradey Park, Llanelli in 1935 saw Johnnie Clay return the best ever bowling figures recorded in a match for the Welsh county. His virtuoso performance came after Northamptonshire opted to take first use of a drying wicket. Their openers, Fred Bakewell and Alex Snowden, had calmly progressed to 47 without loss before Clay had Snowden caught behind by wicketkeeper Tom Brierley. This was the only alarm in Clay's opening ten-over spell, and new batsmen Norman Grimshaw also appeared in little trouble as the Glamorgan bowlers strove to make another breakthrough.

Everything changed as Mercer, nearing the end of an accurate opening spell, had Bakewell caught behind, before Clay, in the space of a dramatic hour and a half, produced a wonderful sequence of deliveries, taking the next eight wickets at a personal cost of just 18 runs. One of Clay's greatest assets was a clever variation in flight, and it was this which saw Ben Bellamy well held by Turnbull at short-leg. All of his remaining victims either bowled or trapped leg-before as the off-spinner completely confused the visiting batsmen.

The wicket had dried out by the time Glamorgan went in, allowing Dick Duckfield and Cyril Smart to each hit attractive half centuries. But it was George Lavis who finished up as top scorer, with a fine hundred full of stylish drives and strong pulls square of the wicket. However, wickets continued to tumble at the other end, and Lavis was relieved to reach three figures with last man Johnnie Clay as his partner.

Largely through the efforts of Lavis, Northamptonshire needed 212 to avoid an innings defeat, yet in just a couple of hours on the Monday evening they subsided to 103 all out. Clay was once again their chief tormentor, completely deceiving batsman after batsman with his clever variations. None of the visiting players scored more than 16 in their second innings, as Clay steadily worked his way through their batting order. It was left to Emrys Davies to wrap up the innings with the final three wickets, but Clay was the hero of this classic match, finishing with the wonderful analysis of 15-86.

Johnnie Clay

George Lavis

NORTHANTS — 1ST INNINGS / 2ND INNINGS

Batsman	Fielder (1st)	Bowler (1st)	1st	Fielder (2nd)	Bowler (2nd)	2nd
A.H. Bakewell	c Brierley	b Mercer	43		b Mercer	16
*A.W. Snowden	c Brierley	b Clay	18	c D.A. Davies	b Clay	12
N. Grimshaw	not out		44	lbw	b Clay	1
J.E. Timms	lbw	b Clay	8	c D.A. Davies	b Clay	7
A.L. Cox		b Clay	0	c D.A. Davies	b Clay	14
R.J. Partridge		b Clay	0	lbw	b Clay	3
D. Brookes	lbw	b Clay	0	lbw	b Clay	10
+B.W. Bellamy	c Turnbull	b Clay	11		b D.E. Davies	5
L. Cullen	lbw	b Clay	0		b D.E. Davies	4
T.A. Pitt	lbw	b Clay	0	not out		13
E.W. Clark		b Clay	2		b D.E. Davies	6
Extras		(B 4, LB 7)	11		(B 5, LB 7)	12
TOTAL			**137**			**103**

FOW: 1-47, 2-70, 3-95, 4-95, 5-99,
6-109, 7-131, 8-131, 9-131

1-22, 2-25, 3-36, 4-37, 5-54
6-67, 7-79, 8-79, 9-85

Bowling	O	M	R	W	Bowling	O	M	R	W
Mercer	25	9	43	1	Mercer	13	3	30	1
Lavis	3	0	10	0	Lavis	3	0	13	0
Clay	32.2	7	54	9	Clay	16	1	32	6
D.E. Davies	16	8	11	0	D.E. Davies	6.2	0	16	3
Smart	3	0	8	0					

GLAMORGAN — 1ST INNINGS

Batsman	Fielder	Bowler	Runs
A.H. Dyson	st Bellamy	b Partridge	36
D.E. Davies	c Bellamy	b Pitt	13
D. Davies	c and	b Partridge	21
*M.J.L. Turnbull		b Partridge	0
R.G. Duckfield		b Pitt	54
C.C. Smart		b Clark	56
G. Lavis	lbw	b Clark	101
+T.L. Brierley	lbw	b Pitt	5
D.A. Davies		b Partridge	17
J. Mercer	c Bakewell	b Clark	18
J.C. Clay	not out		0
Extras		(B 13, LB 15)	28
TOTAL			**349**

FOW: 1-28, 2-73, 3-73, 4-78, 5-164,
6-214, 7-234, 8-299, 9-340

Bowling	O	M	R	W
Clark	20.4	2	49	3
Pitt	32	9	67	3
Partridge	36	6	106	4
Cox	26	7	78	0
Cullen	2	0	21	0

Glamorgan won by an innings and 109 runs

THE SOUTH AFRICANS

8, 10, 11 July 1935 at Cardiff Arms Park

This game witnessed one of the most outstanding recoveries ever made by a Glamorgan side and, in the performance of debutant Wilf Hughes, a quite remarkable start to a career in first-class cricket. The twenty-four-year-old schoolmaster had previously played as a schoolboy fast bowler in Monmouthshire's Minor County side. After leaving Ebbw Vale Boys School, Hughes opted for a life in academia, believing that he was not good enough to play first-class cricket. He subsequently trained to be a science teacher, and subsequently took up a teaching post in Northamptonshire.

The young Welshman started to play club cricket for Kettering and by the mid-1930s he had built up a decent reputation as an all-rounder. As luck would have it, Glamorgan played their Championship fixture in the town in 1935 and, after hearing about Hughes' exploits with both bat and ball, Maurice Turnbull invited Hughes down to the Arms Park for a trial with the county during the school holidays.

Realising that he had nothing to lose, Hughes made his way to Cardiff, and so impressed the watching officials with his pace bowling and crisp strokeplay that he was drafted into the county's side to play the touring South Africans at the Arms Park. It must have seemed like a dream come true for Hughes as he opened the bowling with Jack Mercer, and he delivered an accurate new ball spell. The wicket though was a good one on which to bat first, and the tourists eventually reached the 400-mark, with Hughes having just one wicket to show for his sweat and toil.

Dai Davies (centre) flanked by the two heroes of the South African match – Wilf Hughes (left) and Cyril Smart (right).

The South African tourists, from left to right, back row: R.J. Williams, K.G. Viljoen, E.A.B. Rowan, D.S. Tomlinson, R.J. Crisp, A.C.B. Langton, A.D. Nourse, X.C. Balakas. Front row: I.J. Siedle, C.I. Vincent, H.B. Cameron, S.J. Snooke (manager), H.F.Wade, B. Mitchell, A.J. Bell, E.L. Dalton.

A cigarette card of Cyril Smart. Born in 1898 in Wiltshire, Smart initially played for Warwickshire before moving to South Wales in 1923. He soon developed a reputation as a ferocious hitter of the ball in club cricket, and after some impressive performances for Briton Ferry, he joined the Glamorgan staff in 1927. His big-hitting made him popular with Glamorgan supporters and in 1935 he also created a new world record by hitting Hampshire's Gerry Hill for 32 runs in an over at the Arms Park.

33

But he more than made a name for himself with some clean hitting – and all when Glamorgan followed on after having been hustled out by the Springboks on the second day. Hughes' amazing innings came on the third and final day of the game, which had begun with Glamorgan on 10-4 in their second innings, still the small matter of 249 runs in arrears. Dyson, Brierley and the two Davies – Dai and Emrys – were already out and when Turnbull was dismissed early on the final morning, it seemed that the end was nigh!

But Cyril Smart was in defiant mood and together with Jack Mercer they took the score to 114-7 before Mercer was out, quickly followed by Ted Glover to leave Glamorgan on the brink of defeat. Hughes then strode in and in a quite remarkable hour and a half, he and Smart counter-attacked with such gusto that they added a record 131 for the tenth wicket. Hughes completely belied his inexperience, hitting a remarkable 70* with 4 huge sixes and 6 crisply-timed fours, whilst Smart at the other end raced to a century with a series of sweetly timed fours and one mighty six straight through the plate glass window of a hotel in the road opposite the Cardiff ground.

Much to the delight of the crowd, they were still unbeaten as the umpires removed the bails for lunch, and the pair of batsmen received a standing ovation as they left the ground. The South Africans no doubt felt that the break would interrupt the concentration of the Glamorgan batsmen and, as they dined, they no doubt looked forward to getting back out and polishing off the brave resistance.

But almost as if some Welsh prayers had been answered, rain started to fall during the interval, and as the afternoon progressed, the rain steadily got heavier. By the tea interval, several pools lay on the outfield and the umpires had the formality of calling off play and declaring the match a draw, leaving the South Africans frustrated at the outcome and the Glamorgan supporters gleefully toasting a new hero!

Cardiff Arms Park, as seen from the dressing rooms in the North Stand.

South Africans won the toss and elected to bat · *Umpires: T. Oates and G. Beet*

SOUTH AFRICANS 1ST INNINGS

*H.F. Wade	c and	b D. Davies	139
B. Mitchell	c Dyson	b D.E. Davies	16
E.A. Rowan	c Brierley	b Mercer	153
A.D. Nourse	c Dyson	b Lavis	12
+H.B. Cameron	run out		11
E.L. Dalton		b Mercer	5
K.G. Viljoen		b D.E. Davies	17
C.L. Vincent		b Mercer	0
A.B.C. Langton	c Mercer	b Hughes	23
D.S. Tomlinson	c Brierley	b Glover	8
A.J. Bell	not out		5
Extras		(B 6, LB 6)	12
TOTAL			**401**

FOW: 1-30, 2-281, 3-327, 4-342, 5-346
6-347, 7-349, 8-384, 9-392

Bowling	O	M	R	W
Mercer	27	5	82	3
Hughes	26	5	73	1
D.E. Davies	48	17	90	2
Glover	26.5	3	79	1
Lavis	10	2	23	1
Smart	5	0	31	0
D. Davies	6	1	11	1

GLAMORGAN   1ST INNINGS   2ND INNINGS

A.H. Dyson	c Mitchell	b Langton	18				b Langton	1
D.E. Davies	not out		75				b Langton	0
D. Davies		b Tomlinson	5		run out			3
*M.J.L. Turnbull	lbw	b Langton	1	(5)			b Bell	0
R.G. Duckfield	lbw	b Tomlinson	4	(6)			b Bell	0
C.C. Smart	c and	b Tomlinson	2	(7)	not out			114
+T.L. Brierley	c Wade	b Tomlinson	9	(4)	c Rowan		b Langton	3
G. Lavis	c Nourse	b Tomlinson	8				b Langton	6
E.R.K. Glover		b Vincent	2	(10)			b Langton	0
D.W. Hughes	c Bell	b Vincent	2	(11)	not out			70
J. Mercer	c Viljoen	b Vincent	12	(9)	c Nourse		b Langton	34
Extras		(B 4)	4				(B 12, LB 2)	14
TOTAL			**142**				(for 9 wkts)	**245**

FOW: 1-37, 2-48, 3-49, 4-56, 5-58,   1-0, 2-3, 3-10, 4-10, 5-10,
6-89, 7-109, 8-132, 9-134   6-26, 7-46, 8-114, 9-114

Bowling	O	M	R	W	Bowling	O	M	R	W
Bell	5	0	15	0	Bell	11	2	41	2
Langton	18	8	26	2	Langton	22	5	66	6
Tomlinson	24	4	72	5	Tomlinson	9	0	69	0
Vincent	13.2	3	25	3	Vincent	7	1	36	0
					Mitchell	4	0	19	0

Match Drawn

WORCESTERSHIRE

29, 30, 31 July 1936 at Worcester

Glamorgan have produced a number of England bowlers over the years, but one record has eluded all of them, and indeed the uncapped heroes such as Don Shepherd, Malcolm Nash and Jim Pressdee. This is the feat of taking all ten wickets in an innings – as achieved by Jack Mercer at Worcester in 1936.

Mercer was the mainstay of the Glamorgan attack during the inter-war period and, during his eighteen-year career with the Welsh county, he claimed 1,460 wickets at just 23 runs apiece. Despite his consistency and reputation as one of the best swing bowlers in the country, Mercer never won higher honours and his only major tour was with the MCC to India and the Far East in 1926/27. In keeping with Mercer's colourful lifestyle, he apparently read of his selection whilst at Longchamp races in France!

Mercer's finest hour with the ball came, quite fittingly, during his benefit year, with the veteran seamer having already celebrated his forty-third birthday. The atmospheric conditions on the first morning of the match against Worcestershire at New Road were humid, and overnight rain delayed the start. Even so, the wicket was bone dry, and it looked good enough for Bernard Quaife, the home captain, to have no hesitation in opting to bat first after winning the toss.

Worcestershire were soon in trouble, however, collapsing to 59-6 before lunch as Mercer claimed all six victims, bowling an immaculate length and swinging the new ball lavishly. He

The Glamorgan team, from left to right, back row: Haydn Davies, George Lavis, Cyril Smart, George Reed, Arnold Dyson, Dick Duckfield and Tom Brierley. Front row: Jack Mercer, Viv Jenkins, Maurice Turnbull, Dai Davies, and Emrys Davies.

The picturesque Worcester ground, as seen in the mid 1930s.

The Worcestershire squad of 1936, including all of Mercer's ten victims. From left to right, back row: B.P. King, J.S. Buller, P.F. Jackson, S.H. Martin, F.B.T. Warne, R. Howorth. Middle row: H.H.I.H. Gibbons, B.W. Quaife, Hon. C.J. Lyttelton, R.H.C. Human, R.T.D. Perks. Front row: L. Oakley, C.H. Bull, A.P. Singleton, J. Horton, R.D.M. Evers.

was also assisted by some fine catching in the slips by Cyril Smart, and also Maurice Turnbull at short-leg. The only batsmen to play with any certainty were Roger Human and Sandy Singleton. After lunch the latter tried to hit Mercer off his length, hoping to force Turnbull into making a bowling change. Despite being smashed to the ropes several times by Singleton, the wily Mercer asked wicketkeeper Tom Brierley to stand up to the stumps and soon afterwards had Singleton stumped as he fell out of his ground, defeated by Mercer's swing.

Mercer then added further to his tally, removing Dick Howorth and Reg Perks. With all nine wickets to his name, the fielders realised that Mercer was on the verge of a remarkable club record. Apparently, Emrys Davies, who was bowling at the other end, deliberately sent the balls in his next over wide of the stumps, simply to give Mercer a chance of claiming all ten. The tension started to mount and several half chances from Mercer were spilled as the fielders also desperately tried to help Mercer claim all the opposition's wickets.

After Human had been given a life, it looked as if Mercer would miss out on a place in the club's history, but then Peter Jackson skied the ball into the outfield. George Lavis ran underneath the descending ball, juggled with it for a few heart-stopping seconds, before holding on with an audible sigh of relief echoing all around the ground.

Perhaps the calmest person on the ground was Mercer himself. He just smiled, swung his sweater over his shoulder and turned around to walk back to the pavilion. As his delighted colleagues gathered around, Mercer nonchalantly shook the hands of the batsmen and bowlers and then walked off as if nothing had happened. Rain interrupted play over the next two days, preventing Mercer from adding significantly to his haul. However, the lack of play on the second day was probably a blessing in disguise as the Glamorgan team, and Mercer in particular, had celebrated long into the night!

Jack Mercer

WORCESTERSHIRE 1ST INNINGS   2ND INNINGS

C.H. Bull	c Brierley	b Mercer	22	c Turnbull	b Reed	66	
R.D.M. Evers	c Smart	b Mercer	3	lbw	b Reed	18	
S.H. Martin	c Turnbull	b Mercer	4		b Reed	0	
H.H.I. Gibbons	c Turnbull	b Mercer	2	lbw	b Mercer	8	
*+ B.W. Quaife	c D. Davies	b Mercer	2				
J. Horton		b Mercer	0				
R.H.C. Human	not out		59	(5) c Smart	b Reed	42	
A.P. Singleton	st Brierley	b Mercer	29				
R. Howorth		b Mercer	3	(6)	not out	14	
R.T.D. Perks	lbw	b Mercer	0	(7)	not out	8	
P.F. Jackson	c Lavis	b Mercer	1				
Extras		(B 6, LB 9, W 3)	18		(B 3, LB 3, W 1)	7	
TOTAL			**143**		(for 5 wkts dec)	**163**	

FOW: 1-14, 2-20, 3-30, 4-40, 5-42,   1-58, 2-66, 3-75, 4-127, 5-150
6-59, 7-113, 8-121, 9-121

Bowling	O	M	R	W	Bowling	O	M	R	W
Mercer	26	10	54	10	Mercer	21	2	52	1
Reed	12	2	38	0	Reed	22	3	55	4
D. Davies	6	1	9	0	D. Davies	6	1	15	0
D.E. Davies	7	0	27	0	D.E. Davies	8	3	23	0
					Smart	7	1	11	0

GLAMORGAN   1ST INNINGS   2ND INNINGS

A.H. Dyson	c Howorth	b Martin	14	c Evers	b Martin	6	
D.E. Davies	run out		8	(6) not out		6	
D. Davies		b Perks	1				
V.G.J. Jenkins	lbw	b Jackson	13				
R.G. Duckfield	c Human	b Howorth	5				
C.C. Smart	c and	b Howorth	1	(3)	b Perks	0	
*M.J.L. Turnbull	c Horton	b Howorth	14	(2) c Jackson	b Perks	29	
G. Lavis		b Perks	34	(5) not out		14	
+T.L. Brierley		b Howorth	37				
J. Mercer	c Horton	b Perks	12	(4)	b Martin	1	
G.H. Reed	not out		0				
Extras		(B 7, LB 5)	12				
TOTAL			**151**		(for 4 wkts)	**56**	

FOW: 1-26, 2-27, 3-44, 4-46, 5-49,   1-22, 2-25, 3-28, 4-38
6-54, 7-65, 8-127, 9-151

Bowling	O	M	R	W	Bowling	O	M	R	W
Perks	15	2	38	3	Perks	9	1	24	2
Human	1	0	4	0	Jackson	4	0	10	0
Jackson	21	6	38	1	Martin	6	1	17	2
Martin	9	2	28	1	Howorth	2	0	5	0
Howorth	18.1	8	31	4					

Match Drawn

New Zealanders
31 July, 2, 3 August 1937 at Swansea

Glamorgan recorded two comprehensive victories over the New Zealand tourists in 1937. The first victory, at the Arms Park, had seen Dick Duckfield compile an attractive century and off-spinner Closs Jones take 10-94 as Glamorgan won by 6 wickets. The second match at Swansea resulted in Glamorgan recording one of the most emphatic victories in their first-class history.

Seventeen wickets fell on the first day, with Glamorgan indebted to Emrys Davies for a fighting innings of 58 as the accurate Kiwi bowlers, supported by lively fielding, dismissed the Welsh side for 229. This was well short of what Turnbull had envisaged on what appeared to be a true Swansea wicket, but his new ball bowlers soon put Glamorgan back into the match. In particular, Austin Matthews caused the tourists some problems with his lively seam bowling. He reduced them to 21-3, before the left arm spin of Emrys Davies made short work of their lower order, taking 4-16 as New Zealand subsided to 127 with several of their batsmen falling to reckless strokes.

This turned out to be a fine match for Emrys Davies, as the experienced all-rounder shared in an opening partnership of 157 with Arnold Dyson to put Glamorgan into a commanding position. However, it was left to Cyril Smart to put the game out of the tourists' reach, hitting 3 sixes and 10 fours in a brisk innings which guided Glamorgan into an overall lead of 442.

By the final morning of the game, the Swansea wicket was responding more and more to spin bowling, and who better to exploit the turning surface than Johnnie Clay. The veteran off-spinner took 5-27 as the tourists stumbled to 89-8, and the vocal Glamorgan supporters started to clear their throats in anticipation of an overwhelming victory.

The final rites were delivered, fittingly, by Emrys Davies who took 5-30 as Glamorgan won by 332 runs. This still remains the club's largest ever winning margin, and at the time it was clear proof that the club, under Maurice Turnbull's inspirational leadership, had made huge forward strides. It was their tenth victory of the summer – the most they had ever recorded – whilst Clay's bowling took his tally for the season to 141.

Arnold Dyson (left) and Emrys Davies – a fine opening pair.

Glamorgan won the toss and elected to bat   *Umpires: F. Walden and W.A. Buswell*

GLAMORGAN — 1ST INNINGS

Batsman				2ND INNINGS		
A.H. Dyson	lbw	b Vivian	14		b Vivian	77
D.E. Davies	c Lowry	b Lamason	58	lbw	b Lamason	78
D. Davies	lbw	b Moloney	15	(4) c Lamason	b Moloney	12
W.E. Jones		b Moloney	0	(7) c Gallichan	b Moloney	20
R.G. Duckfield	c Vivian	b Page	16		b Vivian	5
C.C. Smart		b Lamason	37		b Carson	94
*M.J.L. Turnbull	lbw	b Lamason	9	(3)	b Vivian	4
+T.L. Brierley	c Weir	b Carson	38	c sub	b Vivian	15
E.C. Jones	c Moloney	b Page	16	not out		22
A.D.G. Matthews	c Lamason	b Weir	11	run out		9
J.C. Clay	not out		0		b Carson	0
Extras		(B 5, LB 9, NB 1)	15		(B 3, LB 1)	4
TOTAL			**229**			**340**

FOW: 1-22, 2-47, 3-47, 4-79, 5-141, 6-157, 7-162, 8-201, 9-229

FOW: 1-157, 2-161, 3-162, 4-172, 5-180, 6-214, 7-277, 8-313, 9-339

Bowling	O	M	R	W	Bowling	O	M	R	W
Page	11	0	39	2	Weir	5	0	26	0
Weir	9	3	16	1	Vivian	43	16	114	4
Vivian	13	9	7	1	Moloney	22	1	88	2
Moloney	20	3	62	2	Gallichan	8	2	25	0
Gallichan	31	11	56	0	Lamason	18	2	66	1
Lamason	20	10	28	3	Donnelly	2	0	7	0
Donnelly	1	1	0	0	Carson	6.4	3	10	2
Carson	1.2	0	6	1					

NEW ZEALANDERS — 1ST INNINGS

Batsman				2ND INNINGS		
D.A.R. Moloney		b Matthews	0	c Clay	b D.E. Davies	18
W.A. Hadlee	lbw	b Matthews	29	lbw	b Clay	25
+T.C. Lowry	c Brierley	b Matthews	0	c Brierley	b D.E. Davies	16
G.L. Weir	c Smart	b Clay	12	lbw	b D.E. Davies	0
M.P. Donnelly	st Brierley	b E.C. Jones	35	st Brierley	b Clay	16
*M.L. Page	c Turnbull	b D.E. Davies	13	c Turnbull	b Clay	0
W.N. Carson		b D.E. Davies	18	c Turnbull	b D.E. Davies	1
J.L. Kerr	s Brierley	b D.E. Davies	8	(9)	b Clay	4
H.G. Vivian	c Dyson	b Matthews	11	(8) not out		4
N. Gallichan	c Clay	b D.E. Davies	0	(11)	b D.E. Davies	12
J.R. Lamason	not out		0	(10) st Brierley	b Clay	5
Extras		(LB 1)	1		(B 8, LB 1)	9
TOTAL			**127**			**110**

FOW: 1-0, 2-0, 3-21, 4-51, 5-85, 6-104, 7-116, 8-127, 9-127

FOW: 1-40, 2-64, 3-64, 4-84, 5-84, 6-85, 7-85, 8-89, 9-95

Bowling	O	M	R	W	Bowling	O	M	R	W
Matthews	8.3	1	49	4	Matthews	3	0	10	0
Clay	7	0	37	1	Clay	16	1	59	5
E.C. Closs	6	1	24	1	E.C. Jones	1	0	2	0
D.E. Davies	8	2	16	4	D.E. Davies	16.4	4	30	5

Glamorgan won by 322 runs

WORCESTERSHIRE
23, 24, 25 June 1937 at Swansea

By the end of 1937, Johnnie Clay had created a new Glamorgan record taking 176 wickets during the summer in first-class cricket. His finest hour came at St Helen's in the final week of the season, taking 17-212 against Worcestershire – the best ever match figures in Glamorgan's history.

What was even more remarkable about Clay's performance was that the Swansea wicket in Worcestershire's first innings gave the off-spinner little assistance whatsoever. But with skilful flight, change of pace and subtle variations, Clay took 9-66 with only three Worcestershire batsmen getting into double figures against the wily veteran.

The Welsh batsmen then put the wicket into perspective, with Turnbull characteristically leading from the front with a career-best 233, made in a shade over four hours at the crease. Like a good wine, Turnbull's innings got better with time, his first hundred taking 110 minutes, whilst his second came in a further 78 minutes. In all, Turnbull hit 3 sixes and 31 fours, with a mix of strong drives and powerful cuts dominating the bowling in masterly fashion, which put into context Worcestershire's modest first innings efforts. His partnership of 165 for the sixth wicket with George Lavis took just two hours and, when Glamorgan were finally dismissed, they had a lead of 294.

The Worcestershire batsmen made a better fist of things in their second innings, with their openers adding 87 before they were separated. Sid Martin and Bernard Quaife each made half-centuries with some fierce blows, with Martin striking 5 sixes, including three from Clay. But Turnbull was not in the slightest bit worried by this show of aggression, and he had great faith in his wily bowler. The captain simply pushed his fielders deeper as Clay, with a genial smile on his face, gave the ball plenty of air.

Martin eventually holed out to Lavis, and although Quaife remained undefeated, the lower order had few answers to Clay's nagging spin. He finished with 8-146 as Glamorgan strolled to a nine-wicket win, and at the end of the game, in tribute to their wonderful efforts, the spectators at St Helen's made special presentations to the Glamorgan captain and his astute lieutenant for their outstanding efforts, both in this comprehensive victory and the rest of the season, which saw the Welsh county finish in seventh place in the County Championship. This was a huge improvement compared with previous summers and, as the club had never before finished in such a lofty place in the Championship table, it was clear evidence of the headway that the side had made under Turnbull and Clay's guidance.

Johnnie Clay (left) and Maurice Turnbull

WORCESTERSHIRE 1ST INNINGS

						2ND INNINGS		
F.B. Warne	st Brierley	b Mercer	6	(2)			b Clay	39
C.H. Bull	lbw	b Clay	25	(1)	lbw		b Mercer	43
E. Cooper		b Clay	42		c Turnbull		b Mercer	47
H.H.I. Gibbons	lbw	b Clay	2				b Clay	1
S.H. Martin	c Brierley	b Clay	9		c Lavis		b Clay	92
*B.W. Quaife	c Smart	b Clay	2	(7)	not out			55
V. Grimshaw	c Dyson	b Clay	15	(6)	c Lavis		b Clay	2
R. Howorth	c Turnbull	b Clay	4				b Clay	28
+J.S. Buller	c and	b Clay	5		lbw		b Clay	26
R.T.D. Perks	c D.Davies	b Clay	4				b Clay	9
P.F. Jackson	not out		7				b Clay	0
Extras		(LB 2)	2				(B 15, LB 2, W 1)	18
TOTAL			**123**					**360**

FOW: 1-8, 2-40, 3-42, 4-60, 5-66,   1-87, 2-91, 3-92, 4-229, 5-240,
6-93, 7-97, 8-103, 9-107   6-240, 7-291, 8-340, 9-358

Bowling	O	M	R	W	Bowling	O	M	R	W
Mercer	10	1	26	1	Mercer	27	2	87	2
Lavis	4	1	4	0	Lavis	5	0	17	0
Clay	28.5	6	66	9	Clay	34	5	146	8
D.E. Davies	14	5	17	0	D.E. Davies	22	5	48	0
Jones	5	1	8	0	Jones	3	0	9	0
Smart	1	1	0	0	Smart	7	0	25	0
D. Davies	4	1	10	0					

GLAMORGAN   1ST INNINGS

					2ND INNINGS		
A.H. Dyson	c Buller	b Perks	0	lbw		b Jackson	25
D.E. Davies	c Buller	b Martin	8	not out			31
D. Davies	lbw	b Howorth	28				
*M.J.L. Turnbull	c Buller	b Howorth	233				
R.G. Duckfield		b Martin	31				
C.C. Smart	lbw	b Howorth	0				
G. Lavis	c Warne	b Howorth	63				
+T.L. Brierley	c Buller	b Howorth	27				
J.C. Clay		b Jackson	5				
E.C. Jones	not out		0	(3)	not out		14
J. Mercer	c Quaife	b Howorth	12				
Extras		(B 2, LB 8)	10				
TOTAL			**417**		(for 1 wkt)		**70**

FOW: 1-0, 2-14, 3-89, 4-171, 5-186,   1-43
6-351, 7-374, 8-402, 9-404

Bowling	O	M	R	W	Bowling	O	M	R	W
Perks	26	5	115	1	Perks	5	0	14	0
Martin	25	7	78	2	Martin	5	1	22	0
Jackson	20	3	102	1	Jackson	5	1	13	1
Howorth	28.2	6	96	6	Howorth	5	1	12	0
Warne	2	0	16	0	Quaife	1	0	5	0
Bull	0.2	0	4	0					

Glamorgan won by 9 wickets

LEICESTERSHIRE

19, 20, 21 May 1937 at Leicester

This classic match saw a remarkable performance from Emrys Davies, Glamorgan's opening batsman and left-arm spin bowler. In Glamorgan's first innings, Davies shared a record opening partnership of 274 with Arnold Dyson and then, in Leicestershire's second innings, he capped a fine all-round performance with a hat-trick as the home team followed on and lost by an innings. Earlier in his county career, Davies had met with little success and some of Glamorgan's officials had called for his release from the playing staff. However, Maurice Turnbull believed that, with greater confidence, Davies could develop into a leading all-rounder. The influential Glamorgan skipper spoke up on Davies' behalf on several occasions, and Davies repaid his loyal supporter with some outstanding performances with both bat and ball.

The turning point in Davies' career was promotion to opening batsman in 1932. The partnership he subsequently forged with Arnold Dyson proved to be one of the most productive in the club's history, and in this classic encounter the pair shared an opening stand of 274 with Davies hitting 14 fine boundaries in his century. Both of the openers fell within a couple of balls of each other, but Turnbull ensured that the initiative was not lost, with a scintillating hundred in just two hours. His majestic innings contained 4 sixes and 13 fours, and when he reached three figures it was the first occasion in the club's history that three batsmen had scored centuries in the same innings.

Leicestershire got off to a steady start, before both openers fell to the flighted leg-spin of Cyril Smart. Turnbull could call upon a full compliment of spin bowlers in this particular match, as besides Smart's leg breaks, there was the off-spin of Clay and Closs Jones, plus Emrys Davies' slow left-arm deliveries. Indeed, it was Davies and Jones who shared seven wickets between them as Leicestershire were dismissed for 164 and followed on 305 runs behind.

Norman Armstrong and Stewie Dempster offered more resistance a second time around, sharing a partnership of 155 for the third wicket, with captain Dempster making a laconic hundred. However, few of his colleagues were able to offer any lengthy support and, with a substantial lead, Turnbull was able to keep an attacking field and wait for the mistakes to happen. It proved a wise tactic as the last eight Leicestershire wickets fell for just 68 runs. It was during this dramatic collapse that Davies claimed his hat-trick, dismissing George Geary, Herrick Bowley and Haydon Smith. In doing so, he became only the seventh player in the history of first-class cricket to score a century and take a hat-trick in the same match.

Emrys Davies – the 'Rock' of Glamorgan.

Glamorgan won the toss and elected to bat   *Umpires: E. Robinson and J. Hardstaff*

GLAMORGAN   1ST INNINGS

A.H. Dyson	c Dempster	b Bowley	126
D.E. Davies	st Corrall	b Astill	139
*M.J.L. Turnbull	c Berry	b Astill	135
D. Davies	c Armstrong	b Bowley	13
R.G. Duckfield	lbw	b Bowley	1
C.C. Smart	c Berry	b Bowley	33
+T.L. Brierley	run out		10
E.C. Jones	not out		3
J.C. Clay			
J. Mercer			
W.D. Hughes			
Extras		(LB 8, NB 1)	9
TOTAL		(for 7 wkts dec)	**469**

FOW: 1-274, 2-274, 3-298, 4-299, 5-370, 6-413, 7-469

Bowling	O	M	R	W
Smith	44	11	115	0
Geary	38	3	90	0
Bowley	48	8	155	4
Astill	26.3	6	82	2
Prentice	4	0	15	0
Armstrong	2	0	3	0

LEICESTERSHIRE   1ST INNINGS

				2ND INNINGS		
L.G. Berry	c D.Davies	b Smart	24	lbw	b Clay	22
F.T. Prentice	c Turnbull	b Smart	23	c Turnbull	b Mercer	6
N.F. Armstrong	c Smart	b Jones	44	c Brierley	b Jones	73
*C.S. Dempster		b D.E. Davies	35	c and	b Mercer	102
H.C. Graham		b Clay	4	run out		3
H. Riley	c D. Davies	b D.E. Davies	0	lbw	b Clay	9
G. Geary	c D. Davies	b D.E. Davies	6	c Smart	b D.E. Davies	13
W.E. Astill		b Jones	11	not out		7
H.B. Bowley		b D.E. Davies	0	c D. Davies	b D.E. Davies	0
H.A. Smith	c Mercer	b Jones	8	lbw	b D.E. Davies	1
+P. Corrall	not out		0	c Dyson	b Jones	1
Extras		(B 2, LB 7)	9		(B 18, LB 1)	19
TOTAL			**164**			**256**

FOW: 1-52, 2-62, 3-114, 4-119, 5-126   1-17, 2-33, 3-188,4-216, 5-217,
6-140, 7-154, 8-155, 9-159   6-241, 7-241, 8-241, 9-243

Bowling	O	M	R	W	Bowling	O	M	R	W
Mercer	8	1	15	0	Mercer	27	4	53	2
Hughes	11	3	16	0	Hughes	4	0	18	0
Jones	15.3	7	31	3	Jones	27	8	63	2
Smart	11	1	36	2	Smart	6	0	12	0
Clay	18	6	30	1	Clay	23	4	55	2
D.E. Davies	18	6	27	4	D.E. Davies	22	9	31	3
					D. Davies	5	2	5	0

Glamorgan won by an innings and 49 runs

THE WEST INDIANS
24, 26, 27 May 1939 at Cardiff Arms Park

Few sporting heroes were literally much bigger than Wilf Wooller, the Welsh rugby international, Cambridge double blue and highly influential Glamorgan skipper. Indeed, his sporting curriculum vitae read like one belonging to a mythical character from a *Boy's Own* comic, as he had also been in the first Welsh rugby team to defeat England at Twickenham, besides becoming the first Glamorgan captain to lead the club to the Championship title in 1948.

Wooller came down from Cambridge during the summer of 1936 and, during the years before the Second World War, he worked in the coal trade at Cardiff Docks, played club cricket for St Fagan's and rugby for Cardiff. His work commitments prevented him from regularly playing county cricket, but in 1938 he agreed to an approach from Turnbull to play for Glamorgan when the Welsh county were struck by injury.

In typically ebullient manner, Wooller marked his county debut with a return of 5-90 against Yorkshire at the Arms Park, and the following year at the same ground, Wooller made a maiden county hundred against the West Indies. Going in at 152-5, Wooller counter-attacked from the outset, with a ferocious series of hooks, cuts and cover drives. He celebrated his fifty with a huge six into the tennis courts alongside the Arms Park, and went on to reach a century in just two hours, completely wresting the initiative from the tourists. His efforts with the bat helped Glamorgan to 377, and despite two cameo innings from 'Foffie' Williams and Learie Constantine, the Welsh side secured a healthy lead of 124. Peter Judge, their new opening bowler, led the way with four wickets in the West Indies first innings, followed by two more in the tourists' second innings as the West Indies attempted to make 282 to win on the final afternoon.

But it was Wilf Wooller who put paid to any thoughts that the West Indies might have had of victory. He started by claiming two early wickets, and then returned later in the innings to break a spirited partnership between Derek Sealy and 'Monkey' Cameron, that at one stage looked like allowing the tourists to make a fighting comeback. Fittingly, it was Wooller who picked up the final wicket, as Glamorgan celebrated another memorable triumph over a Test-playing nation. The burly all-rounder left the Arms Park to loud applause with figures of 5-69, and the following morning the correspondent of the *Western Mail* suggested that Wilf 'was challenging even Learie Constantine as one of cricket's breeziest personalities.' Not bad for someone with just a handful of county appearances to his name!

An unusual cigarette card of Wilf Wooller.

Haydn Davies

GLAMORGAN — 1ST INNINGS / 2ND INNINGS

Batsman			1st				2nd
A.H. Dyson	lbw	b Williams	1	c Barrow		b Constantine	34
D.E. Davies		b Cameron	25	c and		b Cameron	5
T.L. Brierley		b Williams	9	c Grant		b Martindale	8
*M.J.L. Turnbull	lbw	b Constantine	60	(8)c Stollmeyer		b Constantine	36
D. Davies		b Williams	23	c Grant		b Cameron	26
C.C. Smart	c Barrow	b Martindale	27			b Cameron	10
W. Wooller	c Headley	b Grant	111	c Sealy		b Constantine	14
E.C. Jones	c and	b Martindale	39	(9)lbw		b Constantine	0
+H.G. Davies	c Grant	b Clarke	64	(4)		b Martindale	3
J.C. Clay	not out		2	not out			11
P.F. Judge	c Williams	b Grant	2			b Constantine	3
Extras		(B 5, LB 7, W 1, NB 1)	14			(B 4, LB 2, NB 1)	7
TOTAL			**377**				**157**

FOW: 1-3, 2-25, 3-71, 4-103, 5-152,
6-156, 7-263, 8-366, 9-374

1-14, 2-24, 3-73, 4-73, 5-83,
6-103, 7-103, 8-138, 9-142

Bowling	O	M	R	W	Bowling	O	M	R	W
Martindale	17	0	84	2	Martindale	11	2	26	2
Williams	15	2	44	3	Williams	4	1	19	0
Constantine	13	0	74	1	Constantine	16.1	3	49	5
Sealy	3	0	10	0	Sealy	1	0	1	0
Cameron	9	1	38	1	Cameron	18	5	41	3
Clarke	15	0	97	1	Clarke	4	0	14	0
Grant	2.3	0	16	2					

WEST INDIANS — 1ST INNINGS / 2ND INNINGS

Batsman			1st				2nd
+I. Barrow	c Dyson	b Clay	8			b Judge	0
V.H. Stollmeyer	c Dyson	b Judge	2	lbw		b Wooller	8
H.P. Bayley	run out		12	(5)		b Wooller	1
E.A.V. Williams		b Judge	96	(8)		b Clay	3
C.B. Clarke	c Judge	b Clay	0	(11) not out			4
J.E.D. Sealy		b Wooller	14	(4) c Jones		b D.E. Davies	58
J.H. Cameron	lbw	b Clay	16	c Judge		b Wooller	46
G.A. Headley	c H.G.Davies	b D.E.Davies	20	(3) c H.G. Davies		b Wooller	19
L.N. Constantine	c D.E.Davies	b Judge	63	(6)		b D.E. Davies	19
*R.S. Grant	not out		6	(9) c Smart		b Judge	43
E.A. Martindale	c D. Davies	b Judge	5	(10) lbw		b Wooller	2
Extras		(B 6, LB 5)	11			(LB 4, W 1)	5
TOTAL			**253**				**208**

FOW: 1-7, 2-23, 3-23, 4-23, 5-44,
6-77, 7-134, 8-235, 9-247

1-0, 2-20, 3-41, 4-49, 5-86,
6-114, 7-119, 8-201, 9-202

Bowling	O	M	R	W	Bowling	O	M	R	W
Judge	13.3	0	57	4	Judge	10	1	52	2
Wooller	18	4	57	1	Wooller	13.1	0	69	5
Clay	16	4	59	3	Clay	12	0	53	1
D.E. Davies	10	1	46	1	D.E. Davies	9	1	26	2
Smart	4	0	23	0	Smart	1	0	3	0

Glamorgan won by 73 runs

GLOUCESTERSHIRE
31 May, 1, 2 June 1939 at Newport

The match between Gloucestershire and Glamorgan at Newport in 1939 saw in excess of 1,200 runs being scored on a wicket where almost every bowler, either fast or slow, proved ineffective. The sole exception was Gloucestershire's Tom Goddard, who took 4-45 in Glamorgan's first innings as the Welsh batsmen played a series of rash strokes against the spinner and threw away the advantage that Turnbull had secured in winning the toss on the shirt-front track.

The only Glamorgan batsman to prosper in their first innings was Arnold Dyson, and he was unbeaten on 99 when Goddard bowled Mercer to wrap up the innings. Mercer and Judge each claimed an early victim when Gloucestershire batted, but this only hastened the arrival of master batsman Wally Hammond, the visiting captain.

Hammond proceeded to make a magnificent triple hundred with 2 sixes and 35 fours in a wonderful innings. In particular, the Gloucestershire captain drove with ferocious power and hit one ball out of the ground and through a window of a power station alongside the Rodney Parade ground. Hammond completely dominated the Glamorgan attack, sharing stands of 168 with George Emmett and then 214 with Jack Crapp. The Welsh bowlers wilted under the onslaught as Hammond registered the highest ever score against Glamorgan and, at tea on the second day, he declared the innings with Gloucestershire boasting a first innings lead of 309. In the remaining session on the second day, Arnold Dyson and Emrys Davies restored Glamorgan's morale with an opening stand of 131, as both openers made an unbeaten half-century before the close of play in a day that had seen the small matter of 496 runs being scored for the loss of just two wickets.

By the final morning, the wicket had shown little sign of deteriorating, and Emrys Davies, in particular, was in defiant mood, taking the score to 255 before Dyson was dismissed. Davies remained unperturbed by Dyson's return to the pavilion, and the solid left-hander went on to occupy the crease for the rest of the match, recording what stood for sixty-one years as the highest individual innings for Glamorgan, as the Welsh side also made their largest ever total in first-class cricket. Davies received useful support from Turnbull, with the Glamorgan captain stroking an elegant 77, whilst at the other end Davies continued to work the ball around and reached a maiden double hundred. Later in the afternoon he gained the support of Dai Davies, who realised that his namesake could become Glamorgan's first ever triple centurion. With a special prize also on offer for the season's highest score, Dai Davies generously gave as much of the strike as possible to Emrys in an attempt to allow him to reach 300 before stumps were drawn. However, Hammond also had his eye on the prize for the season's highest innings and, as the match entered its final hour, the Gloucestershire captain employed increasingly more defensive fields as Davies' score mounted. By the last few overs, Hammond had every fielder around the boundary ropes, restricting a quite weary Davies to just singles. When the umpires finally pulled up the stumps, Emrys Davies was unbeaten on 287, a new Glamorgan record, and he had almost single-handedly guided his side to 577-4. There were many loud cheers for the left-hander as he finally walked off the field, and there were also a few jeers for Hammond in protest at his negative tactics, which had prevented Davies from reaching a triple hundred.

Cigarette card images of two of the batting stars of this match – Arnold Dyson (left) and Wally Hammond (right).

Glamorgan won the toss and elected to bat   *Umpires: J. Newman and H. Cruice*

GLAMORGAN

1ST INNINGS				2ND INNINGS		
A.H. Dyson	not out		99	c Wilson	b Lambert	120
D.E. Davies	lbw	b Goddard	34	not out		287
T.L. Brierley		b Scott	9	c Hammond	b Goddard	5
*M.J.L. Turnbull	c Wilson	b Lambert	18	st Wilson	b Emmett	77
D. Davies	c Wilson	b Scott	1	c Lambert	b Sinfield	48
C.C. Smart		b Scott	10	not out		23
W. Wooller		b Goddard	18			
E.C. Jones	c Wilson	b Sinfield	0			
+H.G. Davies	c Wilson	b Sinfield	0			
P.F. Judge	c Neale	b Goddard	3			
J. Mercer		b Goddard	0			
Extras		(B 1, LB 2, NB 1)	4	(LB 17)		17
TOTAL			**196**	(for 4 wkts)		**577**

FOW: 1-65, 2-74, 3-104, 4-114, 5-132,   1-255, 2-265, 3-403, 4-527
6-180, 7-181, 8-181, 9-196

Bowling	O	M	R	W	Bowling	O	M	R	W
Scott	13	0	52	3	Scott	24	1	95	0
C. Barnett	4	0	18	0	Barnett	5	0	32	0
Lambert	14	2	50	1	Lambert	16	0	128	1
Goddard	22.6	7	45	4	Goddard	38	7	123	1
Sinfield	10	3	16	2	Sinfield	36	5	116	1
Emmett	2	0	6	0	Emmett	7	0	51	1
Neale	1	0	5	0	Neale	1	0	11	0
					Hammond	1	0	4	0

GLOUCESTERSHIRE 1ST INNINGS

C.J. Barnett	c D.E. Davies	b Mercer	15
R.A. Sinfield		b D.E. Davies	41
V. Hopkins	c Turnbull	b Judge	13
*W.R. Hammond	c H.G. Davies	b D.E. Davies	302
G.M.Emmett	st H.G. Davies	b Jones	53
J.F. Crapp	not out		60
W.L. Neale	not out		5
+A.E. Wilson			
C.J. Scott			
G.E.E. Lambert			
T.W. Goddard			
Extras		(B 12, LB 4)	16
TOTAL		(for 5 wkts dec)	**505**

FOW: 1-24, 2-52, 3-117, 4-285, 5-499

Bowling	O	M	R	W
Mercer	21	0	105	1
Judge	18	1	83	1
Wooller	23	1	124	0
Jones	9	0	41	1
D.E. Davies	21	2	91	2
D. Davies	2	0	9	0
Smart	6	1	36	0

Match Drawn.

ESSEX

16, 17, 18 June 1948 at Brentwood

Glamorgan's middle-order batsmen strike a rich vein of form in June 1948. The month began with an innings victory over Kent at Gravesend, during which Willie Jones hit a fine 207. After his innings, the modest left-hander from Carmarthen sat in the pavilion at Gravesend and said 'I'll never do it again.'

How wrong he was, as a fortnight later, at Brentwood, Jones recorded another superb double hundred, and sat in the dressing room once again acknowledging the congratulations of his team-mates after an innings of 212★ against Essex and a record-breaking partnership of 313 for the third wicket with Emrys Davies. It was achieved in three and a quarter hours as the Glamorgan batsmen plundered a weary, and quite modest, Essex attack.

In all, Jones batted for four hours, hitting 3 sixes and 22 fours. One of the umpires was Dai Davies, the pre-war Glamorgan veteran and, whilst being impartial, he took great delight at the way Jones and Davies dominated proceedings. As Dai later wrote, the two Glamorgan batsmen 'just went mad and hit everything in sight. Emrys was playing shots all around the wicket with tremendous vigour, and was well into his second hundred, and Willie was not far behind. I knew Emrys would keep going, but Willie started to complain about feeling tired after reaching 150. His knees were always giving him trouble, souvenir of his rugby-playing days, and I knew that Willie was thinking of throwing his wicket away. In Welsh, he said to me "I'm tired, Dai", to which I snapped back, "keep going or I'll hit you on the head with this wicket!"'

Jones duly went on to record a superb double hundred, before Wilf Wooller declared with 586 runs on the board. Essex's woes were quickly made worse as light rain fell to freshen up the wicket. When play re-started, Len Muncer exploited the damp conditions and took six wickets in Essex's first innings, aided by some sharp catching close to the wicket by Watkins, Wooller, Parkhouse and Clift. Even worse was in store when Essex followed on, as Muncer took the first eight wickets, extracting extravagant turn from the damp and worn surface. He then caught Bill Morris off Willie Jones' gentle spin, before bowling Ken Preston to finish with the handsome return of 9-62.

Willie Jones

Len Muncer

Glamorgan won the toss and elected to bat   *Umpires: A.R. Coleman and D. Davies*

GLAMORGAN   1ST INNINGS

D.E. Davies	c Preston	b Dines	215
P.B. Clift		b Preston	14
W.G.A. Parkhouse		b Preston	69
W.E. Jones	not out		212
A.J. Watkins	lbw	b Vigar	4
J.T. Eaglestone	lbw	b Pearce	60
J.E. Pleass	not out		2
*W. Wooller			
B.L. Muncer			
+ H.G. Davies			
N.G. Hever			
Extras		(B 6, LB 4)	10
TOTAL		(for 5 wkts dec)	**586**

FOW: Not known

Bowling	O	M	R	W
Preston	20	0	101	2
Smith	40	12	106	0
Vigar	26	3	123	1
Morris	21	3	94	0
Dines	15	1	77	1
Avery	8	0	38	0
Pearce	5	0	37	1

ESSEX   1ST INNINGS   2ND INNINGS

T.C. Dodds	c Watkins	b Wooller	0		b Muncer	37
S.J. Cray	c Wooller	b Muncer	37		b Muncer	21
A.V. Avery	c Watkins	b Muncer	8		b Muncer	41
F.H. Vigar	c Watkins	b Muncer	9	lbw	b Muncer	1
R. Horsfall	lbw	b Watkins	43	c Watkins	b Muncer	13
*T.N. Pearce		b Muncer	64	c Pleass	b Muncer	4
R. Smith	c Parkhouse	b Muncer	16	lbw	b Muncer	2
+F.H. Rist	not out		20	c Wooller	b Muncer	6
W.B. Morris	c Clift	b Jones	20	c Muncer	b Jones	29
W.J. Dines	c Clift	b Muncer	0	not out		2
K.C. Preston	lbw	b Jones	5		b Muncer	0
Extras		(LB 4, W 1, NB 1)	6		(B 12)	12
TOTAL			**228**			**168**

FOW: Not known

Bowling	O	M	R	W	Bowling	O	M	R	W
Wooller	11	4	19	1	Wooller	10	1	30	0
Hever	8	2	11	0	Hever	5	1	17	0
Muncer	35	8	99	6	Muncer	29.4	8	62	9
Jones	11.4	1	64	2	Jones	16	4	38	1
D.E. Davies	4	0	8	0	Watkins	3	2	3	0
Watkins	4	0	21	1	Clift	5	3	6	0

Glamorgan won by an innings and 90 runs

Surrey

18, 19 August 1948 at Cardiff Arms Park

By the middle of August 1948, Glamorgan's title bid was in full swing, but after some interruptions from the weather, Surrey and Yorkshire were both breathing down the neck of the Welsh county. It meant that the contest between Glamorgan and Surrey at Cardiff Arms Park in mid-August became a vital contest which could decide the final destination of the title.

Surrey arrived at Cardiff with a strong side, but Glamorgan were without all-rounder Allan Watkins, who had been chosen for the England side in the Fifth Test, whilst opening batsman Phil Clift was carrying an injury. Few disagreed with Wilf Wooller's decision to retain the veteran batsman Arnold Dyson in the side, but more than a few eyebrows were raised when Wooller sent out an invitation to another veteran, Johnnie Clay, to join the team for what was arguably the most important game in Glamorgan's history. When the captains went out to toss, the Cardiff wicket was still a little bit moist after overnight rain, but despite the damp, Wooller opted to bat first, believing that the wicket would deteriorate as the game progressed. His decision was vindicated as Dyson and Emrys Davies drew on all of their vast experience to add 91 for the first wicket. Wooller then promoted himself up the order, hitting an aggressive 89 to guide his side to a useful total of 239. Surrey had an hour's batting at the end of the first day, yet even the most optimistic of Glamorgan's supporters could hardly have predicted what would happen in the next sixty minutes. Hever and Wooller took three wickets each with the new ball, before Clay, in the space of an over, took the wickets of McIntyre, Bedser and Laker, to leave Surrey reeling at 47-9 when the umpires called time. In the fourth over of the next morning, Clay finished off the Surrey innings, and Wooller had no hesitation in asking them to follow-on 189 runs behind. Conditions appeared at

first to be easier for batting, with the Surrey openers being in no trouble against the new ball bowlers. But the introduction of spin changed everything, as Muncer and Clay induced another collapse, and at one stage it looked as if the match might even finish before lunch. Bernie Constable and Arthur McIntyre, however, offered staunch resistance to take the game into the afternoon session.

News of Glamorgan's dramatic headway had been buzzing around the nearby centre of Cardiff, and when play resumed after lunch, there were around 10,000 people in the Arms Park ground. Wooller reintroduced Clay into the attack, and the wily veteran soon bowled Laker, before having Clark well caught at short leg by the delighted Glamorgan captain. He then deceived Constable with a slower ball and, soon afterwards, McMahon hit Willie Jones straight to Clay at mid-off, and Glamorgan had recorded an amazing innings victory. It was most fitting that Clay should lead the team off with match figures of 10-65, with everyone associated with the Welsh club realising that they needed just one more victory to become County Champions for the first time in their history.

Wilf Wooller, Glamorgan's influential captain in 1948.

Glamorgan won the toss and elected to bat　　　　*Umpires: T.J. Bartley and B. Flint*

GLAMORGAN　　　　1ST INNINGS

D.E. Davies	c Parker	b Laker	47
A.H. Dyson	lbw	b Laker	51
W.G.A. Parkhouse		b Laker	0
W.E. Jones	st McIntyre	b Laker	1
*W. Wooller	lbw	b Squires	89
J.T. Eaglestone	c Squires	b Bedser	6
J.E. Pless	lbw	b Bedser	0
B.L. Muncer	c Laker	b Bedser	4
+H.G. Davies	c Bedser	b Squires	17
N.G. Hever	not out		1
J.C. Clay	st McIntyre	b Laker	4
Extras	(B 16, LB 1, W 1, NB 1)		19
TOTAL			**239**

FOW: Not known

Bowling	O	M	R	W
Surridge	6	1	11	0
Parker	9	1	24	0
Laker	44.2	10	86	5
McMahon	14	8	33	0
Squires	10	5	11	2
Bedser	30	13	55	3

SURREY　　　1ST INNINGS　　　2ND INNINGS

L.B. Fishlock		b Hever	7	st H.G. Davies	b Muncer	38
M.R. Barton		b Wooller	2		b Muncer	12
H.S. Squires		b Hever	5	lbw	b Clay	9
*+ A.J. McIntyre	st H.G.Davies	b Clay	17	c Clay	b Jones	19
J.F. Parker		b Muncer	6		b Muncer	0
E.A. Bedser	lbw	b Clay	3		b Clay	1
B. Constable	c Dyson	b Muncer	1		b Clay	30
J.C. Laker	lbw	b Clay	0		b Clay	11
T.H. Clark	lbw	b Clay	0	c Wooller	b Clay	0
W.S. Surridge		b Clay	9	not out		33
J.W.J. McMahon	not out		0	c Clay	b Jones	6
Extras			0		(B 5, LB 1)	6
TOTAL			**50**			**165**

Fow: Not known

Bowling	O	M	R	W	Bowling	O	M	R	W
Wooller	6	1	14	1	Wooller	5	1	11	0
Hever	10	2	14	2	Hever	6	1	13	0
Clay	8.2	3	15	5	Clay	27	9	51	5
Muncer	4	1	7	2	Muncer	25	5	61	3
					Jones	5	1	23	2

Glamorgan won by an innings and 24 runs

HAMPSHIRE

21, 23, 24 August 1948 at Bournemouth

The Glamorgan team travelled down to Bournemouth knowing that a victory over Hampshire would be sufficient for them to become County Champions for the first time. The omens looked good as Wilf Wooller won the toss and chose to bat first, but after barely ten minutes play, rain started to fall, and the Glamorgan team spent the rest of the first day in the Dean Park pavilion, eagerly trying to find out details of the progress of Yorkshire, their nearest pursuers, who were playing at Taunton.

These were the days when Sunday was a day of rest for county cricketers, and no doubt several of the Glamorgan side must have said a prayer or three in the local churches that Monday and Tuesday should have fine weather. Their prayers were answered as play began on Monday under clear blue skies. Eleven and a quarter hours playing time remained, so Wilf Wooller told his batsmen to score 300 as quickly as possible, so that he could declare in the late afternoon, and have an hour or so at the Hampshire batsmen.

Everything went as 'The Skipper' wanted – Emrys Davies, Willie Jones and Arnold Dyson all made quickfire half-centuries as Glamorgan raced to 315. Wooller then fired up his bowlers, asking for an all-out attack before the close of play. His bowlers and fielders went out and did him proud as Hampshire slumped to 47-6. All of the home batsmen were harried into making mistakes by some accurate bowling and spirited fielding.

Of all the wickets to fall on that sunny evening, perhaps it was the wicket of Hampshire's opener, Neville Rogers, which epitomised Glamorgan's fire and passion. Gilbert Parkhouse, standing fearlessly at short-leg, flung himself full length to cling onto a firm leg-side shot from the Hampshire batsman, and in the words of John Arlott, watching from the press box, 'with that catch the match was virtually won, because it crystallised Glamorgan's immense psychological advantage which they never lost.'

Tuesday morning dawned bright and sunny again, and Wilf Wooller led his side out in mid-morning knowing that they were poised for a historic victory. Hampshire's first innings soon

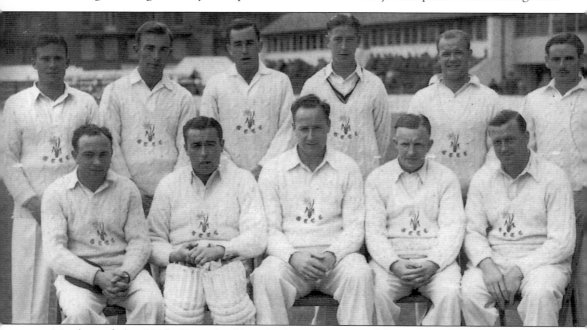

Members of the 1948 Championship winning team. From left to right, back row: Phil Clift, Jimmy Eaglestone, Gilbert Parkhouse, Norman Hever, Allan Watkins, Jim Pleass. Front row: Willie Jones, Haydn Davies, Wilf Wooller, Emrys Davies, Len Muncer.

stern Mail AND SOUTH WALES NEWS

NAL DAILY OF WALES AND MONMOUTHSHIRE

4TH EDITION

J. C. Clay addressing the crowd on behalf of the new county cricket champions—Glamorgan on their arrival at Cardiff General Station last night.

COUNTY CRICKET CROWN COMES TO WALES

Big Cardiff Welcome for Glamorgan Players

By THE SPORTS EDITOR

MEMBERS of Glamorgan County Cricket Team, who arrived back in Cardiff last night after their big victory over Hampshire, which gave them the County Cricket Championship for the first time, received a tumultuous reception at Cardiff General Station, where thousands of people had gathered by 11 p.m.

When the train bringing eight members of the side drew in at the platform, many people rushed forward to shake the players by the hand, and John Clay, in a speech over the station loudspeaker, said he was sorry that the captain, Wilfred Wooller, was not there. He had gone to Lord's to play against the Australians.

It was when the players descended to the station exit that they got their biggest surprise. Thousands of people who had travelled from all parts of South Wales burst into a mighty roar of cheering and then rushed forward to mob the players.

Insisted on Speech

Every vantage point on the ground and above was taken by eager supporters and they insisted in the absence of Wilfred Wooller.

On this occasion Mr Clay said it was "a red letter day" in the history of the county and one which would never be forgotten. "For they are jolly good fellows," and it was not surprising to see tears in the eyes of the majority of those present. It was a great thing

for Glamorgan and the crowd meant the players to realise it.

On the way to cars, which were waiting to take them to the Cardiff Athletic Club, the players passed through a lane of cheering people. One woman from the Docks remarked, "I have just shaken hands with a great cricketer, John Clay."

President's Toast

At the Athletic Club the toast of "Glamorgan County Cricket Club" was proposed by their president, Mr. H. H. Merrett, and the health of the club was drunk in champagne. Speeches by various players followed.

Earlier in the day there had been remarkable scenes at Bournemouth immediately Glamorgan won by an innings and 115 runs. Delighted Welshmen crowded round the pavilion after the match singing "Land of My Fathers" and "Sospan

Championship Table
(Up to and including August 30)

	P.	W.	L.	D.	N.D.	Pts.
Glamorgan	26	13	4	8	1	172
Derbyshire						
Middlesex						
Surrey						
Lancashire						
Hampshire						
Warwickshire						
Gloucestershire						
Worcestershire						
Somerset						
Leicestershire						
Kent						
Sussex						
Nottinghamshire						
Essex						
Northamptonshire						

Essex and Nottinghamshire, whose aggregate scores were equal, each take six points. Includes eight points for a win on first innings in one-day match.

Fach" until Wilfred Wooller and John Clay spoke to them.

As the last ball had been bowled players grabbed stumps and Muncer won the battle for the ball in a typical Test match scene.

Shoals of telegrams continued to pour into the Glamorgan County office from all parts of the country and from the Surrey, Lancashire, and Gloucester teams. There was one also from the Lord Mayor of Cardiff (Alderman R. G. Robinson).

Thus a great day came to a close for Glamorgan—a day which will never be forgotten in the history of Welsh cricket.

Hail the county cricket champions.

A full report of yesterday's play at Bournemouth appears on Page 8.

N.C.B. Stops Old Miners Collecting Coal

By OUR INDUSTRIAL CORRESPONDENT

FOR many years it has been the practice at a number of collieries in South Wales and Monmouthshire to allow old and disabled miners to collect coal from colliery tips for their domestic use.

Now this practice has been banned by the South-western Divisional Coal Board, and at yesterday's meeting of the South Wales area executive council of the National Union of Mineworkers in Cardiff "grave concern" was expressed at the action.

The council decided to ask the National Executive Council to intervene.

The feeling of the Divisional Coal Board is that to allow non-employees on colliery premises would leave them open to many dangers, not the least of which is the question of liability should any of these men injure themselves while collecting the coal.

Despite the urgent recommendation of the executive council, because by a resolution from the coalfield conference some weeks ago, that South Wales mineworkers should support the Saturday voluntary shift, the response has been very disappointing.

On no single Saturday has the output reached the figures attained when the voluntary shift was introduced last November.

The executive council decided to issue a further appeal to the mineworkers to work two Saturday shifts per month at full capacity during "the grave economic crisis through which this country is passing."

Miners Return to Work

The 1,200 miners at Llanbradach Colliery, Glamorgan, who came out on strike on Monday decided yesterday to resume work.

The men struck following wages dispute concerning eight men from whom a bonus shift payment of 24s. was deducted last November.

Mr. Fred Evans, secretary of the local lodge, said: "The men are discontented and are demanding the removal of the manager of the colliery, Mr. Archie Clarke.

"They are going back to work on the understanding that their agent takes up their grievances with the management."

Park Crime Inquiries Extend to Wales

From Our Own Correspondent

NEATH, Tuesday.

THE possibility that John Wood-house, the 27-year-old London barrister, who was found murdered in the grounds of Arundel Castle was engaged to a man whose description is in the hands of Scotland Yard, is now being entertained as a result of investigations undertaken by the police at Neath Abbey to-day.

A nation-wide appeal for information has been completed by Scotland Yard, and following a communication from them Neath police interviewed Miss Edna Adams, a 19-year-old student of Graig Arw, Neath Abbey.

Miss Adams is a third year 'cello student at the Royal College of Music, London, and is now on holiday with her parents, Mr. and Mrs. James Adams.

"I understand she told the police that she was a room mate with Miss Woodhouse and another girl in a London hostel. She went there in May, 1946.

Engagement Ring

Joan had shown her an engagement ring with two inset stones which she kept wrapped in cotton-wool in a little box. When asked why she did not wear it, she replied: "It is my fault," but did not explain.

Before leaving on her fateful journey to Sussex she showed her room mates two photographs of a man—one full length and the other head and shoulders. The man was wearing an open-neck cricket shirt.

Miss Adams has given the police a description of the man in the photograph, and there is a possibility that this is the man to whom she was engaged.

Miss Adams was also able to supply the police with a new photograph of the murdered girl. This was taken by a street photographer when she and Joan were seeing another friend off at a London railway station.

Lorry Examined After P.C.'s Death

Cardiff City Police were yesterday examining a heavy lorry, owned by a haulage firm, which was stopped at Chepstow in the early hours of the morning after Police-constable John Evans had been

Husband of Dorothy Crisp Murdered

SINGAPORE, Tuesday.

MR. JOHN (KILL-BECKER, aged 46, husband of Dorothy Crisp, former head of the British House-wives League, was shot dead here to-day by a Chinese.

Mrs. Becker lives with their two-year-old daughter at Smarden, Kent. She is expecting another child.

The Chinese first called at the offices of Watts and Co. and offered coirs for sale, refused to leave and acted strangely, whereupon Mr. Becker, who is a special constable, phoned the police.

When the police arrived the man had gone, but was found in the offices of John Dickenson and Co.—three floors higher in the same building. Mr. Becker and a police constable tried to handcuff him, and the shooting occurred.—Reuter.

Welsh Ideas May Help Pakistan

Lt.-col. A. J. A. Beck, managing director of the Karachi Trading Estate and industrial adviser to the Pakistan Government, is to visit Cardiff and Glasgow to seek ideas for industrial development in Pakistan.

Mr. H. H. Merrett welcoming J. C. Clay and members of Glamorgan cricket team on their arrival in Cardiff last night after having won the County Cricket Championship.

The Western Mail coverage the day after Glamorgan became County Champions for the first time.

folded and the Glamorgan captain had no hesitation in enforcing the follow-on. With the score on 22, Norman Hever bowled Rogers, but at the end of the over he limped off with a foot injury. His departure prompted a bowling change and, knowing that his spinners were in fine form, Wooller brought on Johnnie Clay and Len Muncer, supported by a cluster of fielders close to the bat.

It seemed as if everything that Wilf Wooller touched in 1948 turned to gold as, within a dozen overs, his spinners had claimed four more wickets. Hampshire captain Desmond Eager then launched a counter-attack, hitting some lusty blows over the in-field, but with the score on 101-5 at lunch, Glamorgan were well on top. There was even better news awaiting Wilf Wooller as he went back to the dressing room, as a telegram had come through from Taunton saying that Somerset had forced Yorkshire to follow on. The county title would therefore be Glamorgan's if they could take the last five Hampshire wickets.

In the second over after lunch, Jim Bailey was run out, and soon afterwards Johnnie Clay started to work his way through the Hampshire tail, dismissing 'Dinty' Dawson, Leo Harrison and 'Lofty' Herman. By sheer coincidence, the umpire standing at Clay's end was Dai Davies, the veteran all-rounder from the inter-war period. It was therefore quite fitting that these two great figures in Glamorgan's history should combine in an amusing way when a ball from Clay rapped Hampshire's last man Charlie Knott on the pads in front of the stumps. Clay led a rousing appeal to which Davies smiled and said 'That's out, and we've won the Championship!'

A large number of Glamorgan supporters had travelled by train and car down to the South Coast, and they mobbed Wooller and his happy team as they walked off Dean Park as County Champions for the first time in the club's history. Twelfth man George Lavis – a fine baritone singer – began a celebratory sing-song in the dressing rooms, and it must have felt like being at the Arms Park and St Helen's, as the supporters gathered in front of the pretty Bournemouth pavilion and sang *Mae Hen Wlad Fy Nhadau* and *Sospan Fach*. The team also assembled on the pavilion balcony, acknowledging the support and joining in with the celebrations.

This was just the start of the party, as later that afternoon the Glamorgan team travelled back by train to Cardiff. Wilf Wooller had been selected to play for the MCC against the Australians at Lord's, so it was Johnnie Clay who led the team off their train when it arrived at Cardiff General shortly after 11 p.m. Thousands of people had gathered at the station to cheer home the victorious team, who then went off to Cardiff Athletic Club for a champagne reception which went on long into the night.

Johnnie Clay and other Glamorgan players read letters of congratulations sent to the club offices after winning the Championship in 1948.

Glamorgan won the toss and elected to bat   *Umpires: D. Davies and P.T. Mills*

GLAMORGAN   1ST INNINGS

D.E. Davies	c Dawson	b Shackleton	74
A.H. Dyson	hit wicket	b Bailey	51
W.G.A. Parkhouse	c Shackleton	b Bailey	2
W.E. Jones	not out		78
*W. Wooller	c and	b Knott	29
J.T. Eaglestone	st Harrison	b Bailey	2
B.L. Muncer	lbw	b Bailey	40
J.E. Pleass		b Knott	0
+ H.G. Davies		b Knott	0
N.G. Hever	c and	b Bailey	18
J.C. Clay	c Herman	b Bailey	2
Extras		(B 13, LB 4, NB 2)	19
TOTAL			**315**

FOW: 1-95, 2-97, 3-164, 4-210, 5-215, 6-277, 7-278, 8-278, 9-303

Bowling	O	M	R	W
Herman	14	4	33	0
Shackleton	17	5	45	1
Knott	42	9	133	3
Bailey	41	8	85	6

HAMPSHIRE   1ST INNINGS   2ND INNINGS

J. Arnold	lbw	b Clay	2	c Dyson	b Clay	16
N.H. Rogers	c Parkhouse	b Wooller	2		b Hever	11
J.R. Bridger	c Parkhouse	b Hever	0		b Clay	18
N.T. McCorkell	c H.G. Davies	b Muncer	34	lbw	b Muncer	12
*E.D.R. Eager	c Wooller	b Muncer	0		b Muncer	39
J. Bailey	c D.E. Davies	b Clay	3	run out		3
G.W. Dawson	c Wooller	b Clay	0	lbw	b Clay	4
+L. Harrison	st H.G. Davies	b Muncer	10	c Muncer	b Clay	5
O.W. Herman		b Muncer	21		b Clay	1
D. Shackleton	c Pleass	b Muncer	0	not out		0
C.J. Knott	not out		2	lbw	b Clay	4
Extras		(B 6, LB 4)	10		(B 2, LB 1)	3
TOTAL			**84**			**116**

FOW: 1-7, 2-8, 3-29, 4-30, 5-47,   1-22, 2-39, 3-48, 4-97, 5-100,
6-47, 7-55, 8-81, 9-81   6-102, 7-103, 8-111, 9-112

Bowling	O	M	R	W		O	M	R	W
Wooller	6	4	8	1	Wooller	6	1	19	0
Hever	6	3	10	1	Hever	4	1	9	1
Muncer	11.5	4	25	5	Muncer	19	9	19	2
Clay	11	0	31	3	Clay	20	5	48	6
Jones	6	2	18	0					

Glamorgan won by an innings and 115 runs

THE SOUTH AFRICANS

4, 6 August 1951 at Swansea

Glamorgan were the only county side to defeat the 1951 South Africans, yet even the most partisan of Welshmen would have been hard pressed to forecast a Glamorgan win when Wilf Wooller's side were dismissed for a modest 111 after being put in on a rain-affected wicket.

During the afternoon session, Glamorgan fought back with Len Muncer taking 5-9 in a fine spell of off-spin, leaving the Springboks at 34-7 at tea. After the interval Athol Rowan and Percy Mansell counter-attacked the bowling, adding 52 in even time for the eighth wicket, before the tourists were also dismissed for 111 to leave honours all square on first innings.

With the St Helen's surface starting to take spin, Glamorgan's batsmen knew that they had to be positive in their approach. For his part, Wilf Wooller needed few invitations to attack the bowling, and if there was anyone who was not going to go down without a fight it was the Welsh county's leader. He hit a typically aggressive 46 and, together with doughty support from Jim Pleass, Glamorgan were able to set the tourists a target of 147.

By tea on the second day the South Africans had reached 54 without loss and the game appeared to be heading away from Glamorgan, as neither of their spinners seemed able to pierce the defence of Springbok openers John Waite or Russell Endean. During the interval, Wooller spoke to his team in the dressing room, cajoling his bowlers for one last effort, and telling them that all that was needed was one wicket, as others would quickly follow.

His words proved prophetic as a quite remarkable passage of play then followed, witnessed by an increasingly animated crowd of 25,000, as all ten wickets fell within the space of three-quarters of hour – and all for just 29 runs. The chief tormentors were Len Muncer, who claimed 4-10, and Jim McConnon, who took 6-10, including a hat-trick. Both were aided by some breathtaking catches close to the wicket, including one by Wilf Wooller at silly mid-on, after deflecting a firm on-drive from Clive van Ryneveld and then clutching onto the rebound inches from the turf.

Even Gilbert Parkhouse, fielding as substitute for Emrys Davies, took two fine catches, and all despite nursing a wrist injury. His second effort was holding on to a huge skier from Athol Rowan, and Parkhouse's catch ended this classic match in Glamorgan's favour. It also prompted a huge invasion of the ground, as Wilf Wooller was carried shoulder-high from the field. The spectators then gathered in front of the Swansea pavilion, sang the Welsh National Anthem, and toasted the players with many glasses of champagne.

The crowd run onto the outfield at St.Helen's after Glamorgan's dramatic victory.

The South Africans won the toss and elected to bat   Umpires: H.L. Parkin and L.J. Todd

GLAMORGAN

	1ST INNINGS				2ND INNINGS		
D.E. Davies	c Van Ryneveld	b Mansell	19	c Endean	b Melle		9
P.B. Clift	c Fullerton	b Melle	0	c Melle	b Mansell		0
B.L. Muncer	lbw	b Rowan	30	(8)	b Rowan		8
W.E. Jones	c Tayfield	b Mansell	13	c Rowan	b Mansell		10
A.J. Watkins	c Mansell	b Rowan	26	run out			11
*W. Wooller	c Nourse	b Mansell	1	c Mansell	b Rowan		46
B. Hedges	c Van Ryneveld	b Rowan	6	c Endean	b Mansell		10
J.E. Pleass	c Van Ryneveld	b Mansell	1	(3) c Fullerton	b Mansell		29
J.E. McConnon	c McLean	b Mansell	4	c Nourse	b Rowan		0
+ H.G. Davies		b Rowan	1	not out			8
D.J. Shepherd	not out		0	c Van Ryneveld	b Rowan		0
Extras		(B 6, LB 4)	10		(B 9, LB 6, W 1)		16
TOTAL			**111**				**147**

FOW: 1-13, 2-39, 3-63, 4-77, 5-89,
6-105, 7-106, 8-108, 9-110

1-3, 2-42, 3-48, 4-63, 5-85,
6-107, 7-130, 8-134, 9-147

Bowling	O	M	R	W	Bowling	O	M	R	W
Melle	5	0	19	1	Melle	9	0	16	1
Mansell	26	11	37	5	Mansell	36	9	73	4
Rowan	21.4	7	45	4	Rowan	28	14	42	4

SOUTH AFRICANS

	1ST INNINGS				2ND INNINGS		
J.H.B. Waite	c Clift	b Wooller	1	c H. Davies	b McConnon		17
+W.R. Endean	c Watkins	b Muncer	13	c Watkins	b Muncer		35
C.B. Van Ryneveld	c Shepherd	b Wooller	4	c Wooller	b McConnon		1
*A.D. Nourse	c Watkins	b Muncer	6	c Watkins	b Muncer		2
J.E. Cheetham	lbw	b Muncer	2	c Watkins	b McConnon		1
R.A. McLean	c Clift	b Muncer	0	lbw	b Muncer		10
G.M. Fullerton		b Muncer	2	(8)	b McConnon		0
P.N.F. Mansell		b Wooller	21	(9) c sub	b McConnon		0
A.M. Rowan	not out		49	(10) c sub	b Muncer		7
H.J. Tayfield	c Wooller	b Muncer	0	(11) not out			0
M.G. Melle		b Muncer	4	(7) c Clift	b McConnon		0
Extras		(B 9)	9		(B 4, LB 6)		10
TOTAL			**111**				**83**

FOW: 1-1, 2-13, 3-27, 4-29, 5-29,
6-33, 7-36, 8-88, 9-95

1-54, 2-54, 3-61, 4-61, 5-68,
6-68, 7-68, 8-72, 9-72

Bowling	O	M	R	W	Bowling	O	M	R	W
Wooller	15	3	41	3	Muncer	8.5	3	16	4
Muncer	23.4	12	45	7	McConnon	10	2	27	6
McConnon	9	3	16	0	Watkins	6	1	12	0
					Shepherd	4	0	18	0

Glamorgan won by 64 runs

DERBYSHIRE
2, 4, 5 June 1951 at Cardiff Arms Park

This classic match saw Glamorgan compile what at the time was their highest total in first-class cricket, with the first six batsmen in the order all passing fifty – a unique achievement in the annals of the club.

The match began with a delighted Wilf Wooller winning the toss on a firm, true Cardiff wicket, and the Glamorgan skipper was delighted to be able to sit back in the pavilion and watch his batsmen prosper against the Derbyshire bowlers. Emrys Davies and Phil Clift shared an opening partnership of 135, before Davies and Parkhouse added 177 for the second wicket.

Parkhouse was in fine form and his sublime century, which included sixteen boundaries, was full of sweetly timed strokes from one of Glamorgan's most graceful ever batsmen. Willie Jones and Allan Watkins then carried on the good work, adding a rumbustuous 113 in a fraction over an hour, as the Derbyshire bowlers tired after a long and quite fruitless day in the field.

On the second morning, Wilf Wooller did not take pity on the Derbyshire attack, and the Glamorgan skipper made a quick-fire half century to take the total past 500. Aware of the club's previous highest total, 586-5 against Essex in 1948, Wooller continued the Glamorgan innings with Len Muncer and Haydn Davies adding some lusty blows to take them past this landmark.

Wooller declared as soon as they had set a new record, and then he let off-spinners Len Muncer and Jim McConnon loose on the Derbyshire batsmen. After their day-and-a-bit of leather chasing, the visitors were quite demoralised, and they duly followed on 376 runs behind. Their captain Guy Willatt then played a captain's innings, watchfully defending, but still punishing the odd loose ball.

There was little support at the other end, however, and McConnon was able to finish with seven wickets in both innings and a fine match haul of 14-153. It confirmed his standing as one of England's most promising off-spinners, having joined Glamorgan in 1950 after a career as a professional footballer. McConnon ended the 1951 season with 136 wickets and, despite a couple of niggling injuries, he continued his meteoric rise to the top echelons of cricket, winning two Test caps in 1954.

Jim McConnon

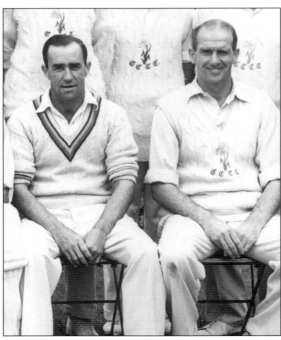

Gilbert Parkhouse (left) and Jim McConnon (right)

Glamorgan won the toss and elected to bat   *Umpires: H. Elliott and J.S. Buller*

GLAMORGAN   1ST INNINGS

D.E. Davies	c Revill	b Morgan	146
P.B. Clift	c Elliott	b Jackson	61
W.G.A. Parkhouse		b Rhodes	107
W.E. Jones	run out		58
A.J. Watkins	c Morgan	b Hamer	72
*W. Wooller		b Jackson	62
J.E. Pleass	run out		0
B.L. Muncer	not out		23
J.E. McConnon	lbw	b Eato	2
+ H.G. Davies	not out		30
N.G. Hever			
Extras		(B 12, LB 9, NB 5)	26
TOTAL		(for 8 wkts dec)	**587**

FOW: 1-135, 2-312, 3-338, 4-451, 5-526, 6-527, 7-527, 8-530

Bowling	O	M	R	W
Jackson	31	8	100	2
Morgan	34	5	133	1
Eato	26	4	106	1
Rhodes	36	10	100	1
Hamer	24	5	98	1
Revill	2	0	24	0

DERBYSHIRE   1ST INNINGS   2ND INNINGS

C.S. Elliott	c Muncer	b McConnon	52	lbw	b Muncer		32
A. Hamer	c Wooller	b Muncer	44	c H.G. Davies	b McConnon		35
J.M. Kelly		b McConnon	46		b Muncer		8
A.C. Revill		b McConnon	29		b McConnon		0
*G.L. Willatt	c H.G.Davies	b McConnon	2	not out			89
D. Smith.		b D.E. Davies	15		b McConnon		20
A.E.G. Rhodes		b D.E. Davies	3	c D.E. Davies	b McConnon		15
+G.O. Dawkes	c Hever	b McConnon	0	c Watkins	b McConnon		19
D.C. Morgan	c Parkhouse,	b McConnon	0	(11) c H.G. Davies	b Watkins		12
A. Eato		b McConnon	10	(9) lbw	b McConnon		0
H.L. Jackson	not out		1	(10) c Jones	b McConnon		4
Extras		(B 7, LB 2)	9		(B 22)		22
TOTAL			**211**				**256**

FOW: 1-96, 2-106, 3-173, 4-182, 5-189,   1-81, 2-81, 3-82, 4-104, 5-139,
     6-197, 7-200, 8-200, 9-202   6-169, 7-205, 8-205, 9-227

Bowling	O	M	R	W	Bowling	O	M	R	W
Hever	15	5	30	0	Hever	9	4	23	0
Wooller	11	1	38	0	Wooller	2	1	4	0
Watkins	11	2	26	0	Watkins	11.1	4	24	1
Jones	4	3	4	0	Muncer	34	11	85	2
Muncer	16	6	18	1	McConnon	44	19	84	7
McConnon	25	6	69	7	D.E. Davies	7	2	14	0
D.E. Davies	15	8	17	2					

Glamorgan won by an innings and 120 runs

MIDDLESEX

10, 11, 12 May 1952 at Lord's

This match saw Glamorgan register their first ever victory at Lord's. Right from early on the first morning, events in this classic match went in Glamorgan's favour, as openers Emrys Davies and Phil Clift added 152 for the first wicket. Denis Compton's chinamen prompted a mid-innings collapse, but Glamorgan still managed to reach 266. Then, in the final hour on Saturday, Don Shepherd, the young fast bowler, bowled a quick and hostile spell with the new ball. The twenty-four-year-old clean bowled Syd Brown with just one run on the board and in a later over repeated the trick against the illustrious pair of Bill Edrich and Denis Compton.

Weekend rain then added to Middlesex's woes as they struggled in damp conditions on Monday morning. Len Muncer revelled in the conditions, tormenting his former employers to return the fine figures of 7.5-3-7-5, as the Welsh county secured a first innings lead of 143.

Alan Moss and Jack Young then struck back for Middlesex, reducing Glamorgan to 28-3, as Allan Watkins strode to the wicket. The England all-rounder had been in many tight situations before, both for club and country, and he drew on all of his experience at Test and county level to launch a bold counter-attack against the Middlesex spinners. His fierce blows extended Glamorgan's lead past the 300 mark, but the Glamorgan innings ended in dramatic fashion as Jack Young took the last three wickets in the space of six balls, as Middlesex were left chasing a target of 338. Watkins still had the bit between his teeth after his fierce strokeplay so, after a brief spell from Wooller with the new ball, the Glamorgan captain introduced him into the attack. It proved a decisive move as Watkins claimed the wickets of both Edrich and Compton in one superb over. At 99-4, and with all of their illustrious run-makers back in the pavilion, Wooller and the Glamorgan side knew that Middlesex's hopes of winning had been dashed.

It was now a case of either a draw or a Glamorgan win, but the latter increasingly became more likely as McConnon and Muncer worked their way through the rest of Middlesex's batting. It was left to Don Shepherd to deliver the *coup de grace*, finishing off the innings by having Jim Sims caught behind and then clean bowling Alan Moss to give Glamorgan a very well-deserved victory, and their first at the headquarters of cricket.

Len Muncer

Allan Watkins

Glamorgan won the toss and elected to bat   Umpires: G.S. Mobey and H.G. Baldwin

GLAMORGAN

1ST INNINGS				2ND INNINGS		
D.E. Davies	c Edrich	b Young	90	c L. Compton	b Young	29
P.B. Clift	c L. Compton	b Young	72	c L. Compton	b Moss	0
W.G.A. Parkhouse		b D. Compton	13	lbw	b Moss	8
W.E. Jones	c Edrich	b D. Compton	10	run out		1
A.J. Watkins		b D. Compton	6		b Moss	65
*W. Wooller		b Young	15	lbw	b D. Compton	37
B. Hedges		b Moss	19		b Moss	26
B.L. Muncer	c Sharp	b Young	27	c Sims	b Young	18
J.E. McConnon	not out		9	c Titmus	b Young	0
+ H.G. Davies		b Moss	0	not out		0
D.J. Shepherd		b Moss	0		b Young	0
Extras		(B 1, LB 4)	5		(B 7, LB 2, NB 1)	10
TOTAL			**266**			**194**

FOW: 1-152, 2-167, 3-179, 4-185, 5-208
6-214, 7-251, 8-265, 9-266

1-1, 2-21, 3-28, 4-70, 5-130,
6-158, 7-194, 8-194, 9-194

Bowling	O	M	R	W	Bowling	O	M	R	W
Moss	21.1	1	65	3	Moss	28	10	44	4
Edrich	10	2	28	0	Edrich	3	0	15	0
Young	32	12	61	4	Young	26	9	63	4
Sims	8	1	29	0	Titmus	10	3	28	0
Routledge	4	0	8	0	D. Compton	9	1	34	1
Titmus	3	0	8	0					
D. Compton	22	4	62	3					

MIDDLESEX

1ST INNINGS				2ND INNINGS		
J.D. Robertson	c H.G. Davies	b Muncer	52		b Shepherd	12
S.M. Brown		b Shepherd	0		b McConnon	40
*W.J. Edrich		b Shepherd	24	c Parkhouse	b Watkins	34
D.C.S. Compton		b Shepherd	1		b Watkins	2
H.R.H.Sharp		b Watkins	5	c and	b Muncer	21
R. Routledge		b Watkins	3		b McConnon	0
+L.H. Compton	c Watkins	b Muncer	15	c Shepherd	b McConnon	20
F.J. Titmus	not out		11		b Muncer	0
J.M. Sims	c Watkins	b Muncer	0	c H.G. Davies	b Shepherd	27
J.A. Young	lbw	b Muncer	4	not out		22
A.E. Moss	lbw	b Muncer	0		b Shepherd	12
Extras		(B 1, LB 6, NB 1)	8		(B 13, LB 3)	16
TOTAL			**123**			**206**

FOW: 1-1, 2-53, 3-55, 4-69, 5-79
6-102, 7-105, 8-109, 9-115

1-18, 2-85, 3-98, 4-99, 5-100,
6-124, 7-124, 8-153, 9-189

Bowling	O	M	R	W	Bowling	O	M	R	W
Shepherd	18	4	38	3	Shepherd	10.2	3	29	3
Wooller	12	3	33	0	Wooller	4	0	15	0
Watkins	17	7	37	2	Watkins	20	5	30	2
Muncer	7.5	3	7	5	Muncer	16	4	34	2
					McConnon	24	1	82	3

Glamorgan won by 131 runs

YORKSHIRE

6, 7, 8 July 1955 at Harrogate

Glamorgan's victory at Harrogate in 1955 was their first ever on Yorkshire soil, and was even more creditable given that they were without Wilf Wooller, had just lost to Hampshire and Leicestershire, and had only just avoided the follow-on in their first innings in this match against Yorkshire.

The home side had batted well on the first day, with Billy Sutcliffe and Doug Padgett dominating proceedings with a stand of 138 for the third wicket. Jim Pressdee caught and bowled Padgett when the Yorkshire opener was in sight of a hundred, but Sutcliffe remained undefeated on 161, hitting 3 sixes and 22 fours. It was not long before Glamorgan were in trouble, subsiding to 40-4 with Willie Jones being the only specialist batsman to offer any resistance against the accurate Yorkshire attack. When the experienced left-hander was finally dismissed by Brian Close for 79, Glamorgan were on 189, and still short of the follow-on.

But, against almost everyone's expectations, Hugh Davies and Don Shepherd then shared a remarkable last-wicket stand of 56, with Shepherd unleashing some furious blows to take Glamorgan past the follow-on target. His brave fusillade eventually ended when Norman Yardley recalled Philip Hodgson into the attack, and the opening bowler had Shepherd caught behind by Jimmy Binks for 48.

Despite this tail-end resistance, Yorkshire still had a first innings lead of 136 and by the second evening they had extended their lead past the 300 mark, thanks to some aggressive blows from Vic Wilson and, for the second time in the match, Doug Padgett. Norman Yardley eventually set Glamorgan a target of 334 on the final day and, with spinner Johnnie Wardle taking the first four wickets, a Yorkshire victory looked on the cards.

Glamorgan's fortunes then took a definite swing for the better, as Jim Pleass was dropped before he had scored. The thirty-two-year-old batsman from Cardiff prospered from this life, and he led the run chase with useful support from Jim McConnon and Jim Pressdee. The Yorkshire bowlers started to tire as Pleass got closer and closer to a maiden century, and right-hander was at the crease when the winning runs were made – and all with just 20 minutes to spare – to give Glamorgan one of their most historic and unlikely victories.

Jim Pleass

Gilbert Parkhouse

Yorkshire won the toss and elected to bat   *Umpires: T.W. Spencer and A. Skelding*

YORKSHIRE   1ST INNINGS

F.A. Lowson	st H.G. Davies	b McConnon	15		b H.D.Davies	23	
D.E.V. Padgett	c and	b Pressdee	96	c Shepherd	b Jones	64	
J.V. Wilson		b Watkins	4		b Watkins	81	
W.H.H. Sutcliffe	not out		161		b McConnon	7	
W. Watson		b Pressdee	0	not out		15	
D.B. Close		b Shepherd	31				
*N.W.D. Yardley	c H.D. Davies	b Watkins	25				
R. Illingworth	not out		33				
J.H. Wardle							
+J.G. Binks							
P. Hodgson							
Extras		(B 2, LB 11, NB 3)	16		(B 1, LB 4, NB 2)	7	
TOTAL		(for 6 wkts dec)	**381**		(for 4 wkts dec)	**197**	

FOW: 1-37 ,2-48, 3-186, 4-188, 5-257,   1-73, 2-117, 3-128, 4-197
6-297

Bowling	O	M	R	W	Bowling	O	M	R	W
Shepherd	29	6	77	1	Shepherd	10	1	42	0
H.D. Davies	23	1	82	0	H.D. Davies	10	0	78	1
McConnon	20	4	43	1	McConnon	6	0	37	1
Watkins	24	3	108	2	Watkins	0.4	0	3	1
Pressdee	13	2	55	2	Jones	7	0	30	1

GLAMORGAN   1ST INNINGS   2ND INNINGS

W.G.A. Parkhouse	c Watson	b Wardle	20	c Wilson	b Wardle	80	
B.R. Edrich	c Wilson.	b Close	5	c Close	b Wardle	21	
B. Hedges	c Padgett.	b Yardley	3	c Watson	b Wardle	7	
W.E. Jones	c Illingworth	b Close	79	c Binks	b Wardle	37	
J.E. Pleass	c Watson	b Wardle	4 (6)		not out	102	
A.J. Watkins	c Yardley	b Illingworth	18 (5)	lwb	b Close	4	
J.S. Pressdee	c Watson	b Illingworth	20 (8)	not out		33	
J.E. McConnon	c Sutcliffe	b Wardle	37 (7)	lbw	b Illingworth	28	
*+ H.G. Davies	c Binks	b Wardle	0				
H.D. Davies	not out		6				
D.J. Shepherd	c Binks	b Hodgson	48				
Extras		(B 1, LB 4)	5		(B 10, LB 12)	22	
TOTAL			**245**		(for 6 wkts)	**334**	

FOW: 1-10, 2-24, 3-28, 4-40, 5-144,   1-53, 2-75, 3-145, 4-154, 5-166
6-176, 7-189, 8-189, 9-189   6-263

Bowling	O	M	R	W	Bowling	O	M	R	W
Hodgson	17.4	4	49	1	Hodgson	12	0	51	0
Close	23	6	66	2	Close	30	13	75	1
Wardle	35	12	102	4	Wardle	38	9	110	4
Yardley	6	4	7	1	Yardley	2	0	10	0
Illingworth	19	11	16	2	Illingworth	25.3	6	66	1

Glamorgan won by 4 wickets

The Indians

16, 18, 19 May 1959 at Cardiff Arms Park

Injuries and illness prevented Glamorgan from fielding a very experienced side for their match at the Arms Park in May 1959 against the Indian tourists. Without captain Wilf Wooller, it was left to stand-in leader Allan Watkins to lead the Welsh county to a remarkable win.

The Glamorgan batting order had an unfamiliar look about it, and in the absence of the experienced pairing of Gilbert Parkhouse and Bernard Hedges, young left-hander Alan Jones opened the batting with Peter Walker, whilst Jim Pressdee was promoted to number three. The twenty-five-year-old Pressdee responded to the challenge with a quite superb maiden century, boldly hitting 15 fours and a six. His dominance can be gauged by the fact that the next highest score was 19 by Alan Jones.

When the Indians batted later in the day, they also found life difficult on the Arms Park wicket, and none of their batsmen passed fifty as they were contained by the accurate left-arm bowling of Peter Walker and teased by the clever off-cutters of Don Shepherd. Their efforts gave Glamorgan a valuable lead of 70 and, when Glamorgan batted again, Allan Watkins played a captain's innings with an attractive 61.

Watkins had been quite fortunate, having been dropped off his first ball, and the tourists were to rue this costly miss as Watkins and McConnon shared a useful stand of 78 for the sixth wicket. Don Shepherd then rubbed salt into the Indians' wounds by hitting a quickfire 42 in a mere twenty minutes, including 3 huge sixes and 4 fours.

The net result was that India needed 294 to win and, after losing two early wickets to Peter Walker, Datta Gaekwad and Chandra Borde shared a partnership of 129 to put the tourists in a quite useful position at 193-3. The equation was now 101 runs to win with seven wickets in hand, but Gaekwad was run out, and Borde was superbly caught by Peter Walker at short-leg off McConnon's bowling.

Soon after Jayasinghrao Ghorpade was bowled first ball by Don Ward and Nari Contractor was caught by Watkins off Ward. With the scoreboard reading 199-7, the match had swung decidedly in Glamorgan's favour. There were some fierce blows from Kripal Singh, before Peter Walker brought off another fine catch close to the wicket. McConnon then finished off the Indian tailenders, and Glamorgan were able to celebrate a fine victory by 51 runs.

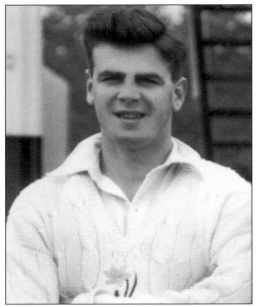

Jim Pressdee

Peter Walker

GLAMORGAN — 1ST INNINGS / 2ND INNINGS

Batsman	1st fielder	1st bowler	R	2nd fielder	2nd bowler	R
A. Jones	c Ghorpade	b Desai	19		b Borde	28
P.M. Walker	c Tamhane	b Desai	5		b Desai	1
J.S. Pressdee	c Contractor	b Borde	113		b Muddiah	19
D.J. Ward	c Tamhane	b Muddiah	14	c Kripal Singh	b Muddiah	1
*A.J. Watkins	lbw	b Muddiah	0	c and	b Desai	61
L.N. Devereux	run out		1	c Kripal Singh	b Muddiah	3
J.E. McConnon	c Contractor	b Muddiah	15	lbw	b Muddiah	52
+D.G.L. Evans	c and	b Borde	6	st Tamhane	b Muddiah	2
H.D. Davies	lbw	b Borde	0	c sub	b Muddiah	0
D.J. Shepherd	c Muddiah	b Borde	0	c Umrigar	b Borde	42
F.J. Clarke	not out		5	not out		0
Extras		(B 4)	4		(B 12, LB 2)	14
TOTAL			182			223

FOW: 1-12, 2-35, 3-74, 4-74, 5-82, 6-104, 7-135, 8-135, 9-135

FOW: 1-1, 2-40, 3-42, 4-72, 5-95, 6-173, 7-177, 8-181, 9-217

Bowling	O	M	R	W	Bowling	O	M	R	W
Desai	14	5	31	2	Desai	13	4	34	2
Surendranath	12	2	38	0	Surendranath	6	2	5	0
Muddiah	21	4	66	3	Muddiah	27	10	79	6
Ghorpade	5	0	26	0	Borde	21.4	5	65	2
Borde	10.4	4	17	4	Umrigar	11	4	26	0

THE INDIANS — 1ST INNINGS / 2ND INNINGS

Batsman	1st fielder	1st bowler	R	2nd fielder	2nd bowler	R
P.K. Roy	lbw	b Shepherd	10	c McConnon	b Walker	11
N.J. Contractor	c Evans	b Clarke	2	(8) c Watkins	b Ward	0
*P.R. Umrigar		b Shepherd	35	c Walker	b McConnon	10
D.K. Gaekwad	lbw	b Walker	26	run out		63
C.G. Borde	c Walker	b Davies	13	c Walker	b McConnon	64
J.M. Ghorpade	run out		0		b Ward	0
Kripal Singh	c McConnon	b Walker	3	c Walker	b Shepherd	26
+N.S. Tamhane	c Devereux	b Shepherd	5	(2) c and	b Walker	34
Surendranath	not out		8	c Watkins	b McConnon	14
R.B. Desai	c Evans	b Walker	0	c Jones	b McConnon	8
V.M. Muddiah		b Shepherd	3	not out		0
Extras		(B 4, NB 3)	7		(B 12)	12
TOTAL			112			242

FOW: 1-3, 2-39, 3-49, 4-72, 5-73, 6-89, 7-96, 8-102, 9-103

FOW: 1-23, 2-54, 3-64, 4-193, 5-193, 6-193, 7-199, 8-234, 9-234

Bowling	O	M	R	W	Bowling	O	M	R	W
Clarke	10	5	26	1	Clarke	3	0	9	0
Davies	16	4	38	1	Davies	4	2	3	0
Shepherd	21.5	7	34	4	Shepherd	18	6	37	1
Walker	9	6	7	3	Walker	21	4	79	2
					McConnon	31.4	9	72	4
					Ward	11	5	30	2

Glamorgan won by 51 runs

SOMERSET

22 May 1963 at Cardiff Arms Park

One-day cricket was introduced into the county calendar in 1963, with the seventeen teams taking part in a 65-overs-a-side contest, sponsored by Gillette. Glamorgan's inaugural match in the new competition took place against Somerset at the Arms Park on 22 May, and the Welsh county duly won a closely fought game, thanks to a fine century from Bernard Hedges and some fiery new ball bowling by Jeff Jones.

However, a Glamorgan defeat had looked the more likely result after the Welsh county faltered in the opening overs. Ken Palmer dismissed Alwyn Harris, whilst Fred Rumsey caught and bowled Alan Jones to leave Glamorgan on 11-2. But Tony Lewis and Bernard Hedges then added exactly 100 for the third wicket to wrest the initiative back in Glamorgan's favour.

Despite the departure of Lewis for 40, and the subsequent loss of three further wickets for just 7 runs, Hedges kept the scoreboard ticking over with deft placement, plus the occasional boundary. He received valiant support from wicketkeeper Eifion Jones and all-rounder Hamish Miller, and the Pontypridd-born batsman eventually reached a well-deserved century shortly before the end of Glamorgan's 65 overs.

It was then the turn of left-arm quickie Jeff Jones to take centre stage as Somerset chased a target of 208. The young pace bowler from Llanelli dismissed the dangerous Roy Virgin and West Indian Peter Wight in a hostile opening spell, before Hedges' gentle medium pace accounted for Colin Atkinson and Australian Bill Alley. Jones returned to clean-bowl Merv Kitchen for 25 and, after Jim Pressdee had taken the wickets of Chris Greetham, Ken Palmer and Harold Stephenson, Somerset were teetering on the verge of defeat at 121-8.

Brian Langford and David Doughty then shared a spirited partnership for the ninth wicket, adding 75 runs in rapid time. When Langford reached a well made half-century, it looked as if Somerset might pull off a quite remarkable victory – but he was well caught in the deep by Jim Pressdee and in the following over Doughty was dismissed to give Glamorgan a hard-earned victory by 10 runs. It had been a highly entertaining contest, as well as being a good way to launch the new competition, and after his all-round contributions with both bat and ball, Bernard Hedges deservedly won the man of the match cheque for £50.

Bernard Hedges

Jeff Jones

GLAMORGAN INNINGS

A. Harris	c Virgin	b Palmer	6
A. Jones	c and	b Rumsey	5
*A.R. Lewis	c Alley	b Doughty	40
B. Hedges	not out		103
J.S. Pressdee		b Rumsey	16
A. Rees		b Rumsey	0
+D.G.L. Evans		b Rumsey	0
W.D. Slade		b Palmer	0
E.W. Jones	c Stephenson	b Palmer	16
H.D.S. Miller	not out		13
I.J. Jones			
Extras		(B 2, LB 4, W 1, NB 1)	8
TOTAL		(for 8 wickets)	**207**

FOW: 1-6, 2-11, 3-111, 4-146, 5-152,
6-152, 7-153, 8-187

Bowling	O	M	R	W
Palmer	15	2	39	3
Rumsey	15	6	24	4
Alley	15	1	49	0
Langford	2	0	10	0
Greetham	11	0	46	0
Doughty	7	0	31	1

SOMERSET INNINGS

C.R.M. Atkinson		b Hedges	31
R.T. Virgin	c Lewis	b I.J. Jones	1
P.B. Wight	c Hedges	b I.J. Jones	11
W.E. Alley	c A. Jones	b Hedges	19
M.J. Kitchen		b I.J. Jones	25
C.H.M. Greetham	c Hedges	b Pressdee	26
K.E. Palmer	c Evans	b Pressdee	1
*+ W.H. Stephenson	c Lewis	b Pressdee	4
B.A. Langford	c Pressdee	b Miller	56
D.G. Doughty	c I.J. Jones	b Evans	20
F.E. Rumsey	not out		0
Extras		(LB 1, NB 2)	3
TOTAL			**197**

FOW: 1-3, 2-28, 3-64, 4-65, 5-107,
6-116, 7-121, 8-121, 9-196

Bowling	O	M	R	W
I.J. Jones	15	5	34	3
Evans	8.2	1	37	1
Miller	10	0	31	1
Hedges	8	5	17	2
Slade	7	2	29	0
Pressdee	14	4	46	3

Glamorgan won by 10 runs

THE AUSTRALIANS

1, 3, 4 August 1964 at Swansea

In 1964 Glamorgan, under the captaincy of Ossie Wheatley, defeated the Australians for the first time in their history. This victory was staged in front of an enormous, and partisan, crowd at St Helen's over the August Bank Holiday, and all despite Glamorgan fielding a side which had an unfamiliar and inexperienced look about it.

Euros Lewis opened the batting with Alan Jones, Billy Slade came into the middle order, reserve wicketkeeper Eifion Jones took over behind the stumps, and young West Indian pace bowler Tony Cordle opened the bowling instead of Jeff Jones. Even the most ardent of Glamorgan supporters could not have predicted the manner in which this young side would record a famous victory.

Ossie Wheatley won the toss and on the slow, bare Swansea wicket, his batsmen then struggled against the lively Australian attack. Alan Jones drew on his experience of playing State cricket in Australia, and the gritty left-hander launched the innings in an aggressive way. Peter Walker and Alan Rees chipped in with useful contributions of 41 and 48, whilst Don Shepherd also weighed in with a quick-fire 24 to see Glamorgan to their total of 197.

It seemed on the face of it a modest score, but a shower in late-afternoon had dampened the wicket, just to the liking of Don Shepherd and Jim Pressdee. The two spinners proved almost unplayable, even to Bill Lawry, fresh from his 106 in the Fourth Test at Old Trafford. He fell to Don Shepherd for just 7, to the accompaniment of a loud cheer from the crowd. However, an even louder roar occurred a few overs later when Jim Pressdee bowled Bobby Simpson for just 2 – this was clearly a fine achievement, given the fact that the Australian skipper had made 311 at Old Trafford.

The tourists had collapsed to 39-6 by the time stumps were drawn at the end of a very dramatic day, and the pubs all over South Wales that Saturday night, as well as on Sunday, were full of talk about a Welsh victory. The National Eisteddfod was being held just down the road from the Swansea ground, and on the Saturday night and Sunday the tourists visited the Welsh festival of music, drama and culture. If any of the Australian tourists had been in any doubts, their visit to the Eisteddfod proved that they were playing in a most patriotic area.

Alan Jones (right) talks to Australian fast bowler Graham McKenzie before play.

Two great Glamorgan servants – Tony Lewis (left) and Don Shepherd (right).

A crowd of around 25,000 crammed themselves into the famous St Helen's ground on Bank Holiday Monday and, right from the very first ball, there was an air of expectancy and Celtic fervour, more akin to a Welsh rugby international. However, Tom Veivers had other ideas and, mixing caution with aggression, he led a brave fightback with Johnny Martin. However, Martin's resistance was eventually bowled by Don Shepherd, and further wickets followed as the Australians were dismissed for just 101, to give the young Glamorgan side an invaluable lead.

Although the weather was now set fair, the Swansea wicket was still responding to spin and only Tony Lewis and Alan Rees really looked comfortable, especially against the leg-spin of Bobby Simpson. His skilfully flighted bowling saw Glamorgan collapse from 126-4 to 172 all out. The equation therefore was that Australia needed 268 to win and preserve their unbeaten tour record.

With an hour and a half remaining, plus all of the final day, Simpson opened the second innings alongside Bill Lawry. The pair launched the run-chase in a watchful way, with both batsmen being prepared to use their feet against the Glamorgan spinners and make some carefully controlled strokes. They had taken the score to 59 when Simpson fell to a fine catch at silly mid-off by Peter Walker off Don Shepherd's bowling, and the day's play ended with the tourists on 75-1.

This meant that 193 runs were needed on Tuesday, with the Australians knowing that they could continue to play in a quiet way as they had all day to pursue their target. For their part, Glamorgan needed quick wickets and, in a shade over half an hour, the Welsh prayers were answered as Shepherd took two wickets in his opening six overs, whilst the dangerous Norman

71

O'Neill also fell to a superb running catch by Tony Lewis.

With the Swansea scoreboard reading 92-4, Glamorgan had regained the initiative, but opener Bill Lawry was still at the crease and in a most obdurate mood. He continued to stubbornly defend, whilst Tom Veivers counter-attacked for the second time in the match. Veivers hit both spinners for huge sixes and, with Lawry looking in no trouble at the other end, it seemed as if Glamorgan's grip on the match was starting to loosen.

The pair had added 77 in 90 minutes when Veivers went for one shot too many against Pressdee, and was bowled to the accompaniment of a mighty roar from the crowd. Wicketkeeper Barry Jarman then gave Lawry useful support until Lawry, after almost five hours at the crease, pulled a long hop from Jim Pressdee straight into the hands of Alan Rees at mid-wicket.

The buzz of expectation grew louder as the crestfallen Lawry trudged off the ground, and his departure signalled the end of the Australian resistance, as Shepherd and Pressdee worked their way through the tail. Shepherd, in particular, was in magnificent form, taking, in all, five wickets in a marathon spell of controlled off-spin. The final hour of his spell saw him overcome both cramp and the last of the Australian batsmen, as the final four wickets fell for 25 runs.

It was Jim Pressdee who took the last Australian wicket when Neil Hawke was caught by wicketkeeper Eifion Jones. The crowd ran onto the field to applaud their heroes and it seemed as if half of Wales surged across the St Helen's outfield to join in with the ecstatic celebrations in the pavilion. Champagne corks popped, speeches were made and the songs grew louder as it became clear that this was not just a victory for Glamorgan, for it was a day when Wales had won!

The players who beat the 1964 Australians. Front to left, back row: Alan Rees, Eifion Jones, Tony Cordle, Billy Slade, Gwyn Hughes (twelfth man), Euros Lewis, Alan Jones. Front row: Jim Pressdee, Don Shepherd, Ossie Wheatley, Tony Lewis, Peter Walker.

Glamorgan won the toss and elected to bat 　　*Umpires: W.H. Copson and F. Jakeman*

GLAMORGAN

1ST INNINGS				2ND INNINGS			
A. Jones	c Simpson	b Martin	33	c Connolly	b Martin	15
E.J. Lewis	c Simpson	b Veivers	7		b Hawke	11
A.R. Lewis	c Hawke	b Veivers	0	c Connolly	b Veivers	36
P.M. Walker		b Hawke	41	c and	b Veivers	9
J.S. Pressdee		b Martin	6	st Jarman	b Simpson	24
A.H.M. Rees	c Simpson	b Hawke	48	c Jarman	b Simpson	47
W.J. Slade	not out		14	c Connolly	b Simpson	9
+ E.W. Jones	c Connolly	b Veivers	0		b Veivers	4
A.E. Cordle	c Sellers	b Veivers	6	c Potter	b Simpson	6
D.J. Shepherd	c Martin	b Veivers	24	not out		9
*O.S. Wheatley	c Redpath	b Hawke	11	c O'Neill	b Simpson	1
Extras		(LB 6, W 1)	7		(LB 1)	1
TOTAL			**197**			**172**

FOW: 1-42, 2-46, 3-50, 4-62, 5-130　　1-13, 2-49, 3-67, 4-74, 5-126,
6-147, 7-150, 8-156, 9-182　　6-152, 7-152, 8-162, 9-171

Bowling	O	M	R	W		O	M	R	W
Connolly	6	1	22	0	Connolly	3	2	6	0
Hawke	26.1	8	51	3	Hawke	15	3	30	1
Veivers	28	11	85	5	Veivers	28	6	65	3
Martin	7	0	31	2	Martin	8	2	25	1
Simpson	1	0	1	0	Simpson	14.1	4	33	5
Sellers	13	6	12	0					

AUSTRALIANS

1ST INNINGS				2ND INNINGS			
W.M. Lawry	c Slade	b Shepherd	7	c Rees	b Pressdee	64
I.R. Redpath	c Walker	b Pressdee	6	lbw	b Shepherd	5
N.C. O'Neill	st E. Jones	b Pressdee	0	c A. Lewis	b E. Lewis	14
J. Potter	c E. Jones	b Pressdee	2		b Shepherd	0
*R.B. Simpson		b Pressdee	2	c Walker	b Shepherd	32
+B.N. Jarman	c Slade	b Shepherd	4	c E. Jones	b Pressdee	34
T.R. Veivers	c E. Lewis	b Pressdee	51		b Pressdee	54
J.W. Martin		b Shepherd	12	c Pressdee	b Shepherd	6
N.J.N. Hawke	c E. Jones	b Pressdee	0	c E. Jones	b Pressdee	1
R.H.D. Sellers	lbw	b Shepherd	4	c Slade	b Shepherd	4
A.N. Connolly	not out		0	not out		0
Extras		(B 9, LB 1, W 1, NB 2)	13		(B 12, LB 4, W 0, NB 2)	18
TOTAL			**101**			**232**

FOW: 1-15, 2-15, 3-17, 4-21, 5-21,　　1-59, 2-80, 3-88, 4-92, 5-169,
6-39, 7-65, 8-90, 9-95　　6-207, 7-217, 8-228, 9-232

Bowling	O	M	R	W		O	M	R	W
Wheatley	4	3	1	0	Wheatley	5	1	11	0
Cordle	5	1	7	0	Cordle	7	1	14	0
Shepherd	17	12	22	4	Shepherd	52	29	71	5
Pressdee	15.2	5	58	6	Pressdee	28.1	6	65	4
					E. Lewis	26	13	51	1
					Slade	1	0	2	0

Glamorgan won by 36 runs

LEICESTERSHIRE
28, 29, 30 July 1965 at Ebbw Vale

Between 1946 and 1983 Glamorgan played 24 Championship matches at Ebbw Vale, the Monmouthshire steel and mining town, high up in the Ebbw Valley. According to local legend, the square at the Eugene Cross Park ground lay only a few metres above some of the lucrative coal seams and there were stories, possibly apocryphal, of batsmen tapping down the wicket and then hearing a banging noise coming up from miners underground!

It was at Ebbw Vale that Glamorgan beat Leicestershire in a classic match in 1965, foreshortened by six hours after a mix of persistent rain and heavy showers on the first two days. Between the storms, Alan Jones and Peter Walker shared a third-wicket partnership of 173 in a fraction under four hours, before half-centuries from Leicestershire's Maurice Hallam and Clive Inman guided the visitors into a first innings lead.

With the rain clouds still hanging around on the final day, Glamorgan captain Ossie Wheatley knew that his only chance of winning the game would be for his batsmen to go for quick runs and then, weather permitting, leave the visitors a target in the afternoon. Tony Lewis and Peter Walker followed their captain's instructions to the letter with a rapid second-wicket partnership of 83 in just an hour. Alan Rees then chipped in with some furious strokeplay, and Ossie Wheatley was able to declare with two hours remaining and challenge Leicestershire to score 149 in the final 110 minutes. However, their second innings only lasted for 80 minutes as Leicestershire were bowled out for 33 – the lowest ever Championship total made against the Welsh county. Their tormentor-in-chief was Don Shepherd, and the cunning off-spinner induced a remarkable collapse after Ossie Wheatley and Jeff Jones had taken the first two wickets. In the space of just ten overs, Shepherd worked his way through the rest of the innings, and revelled in the damp conditions, extracting sharp turn and bounce, to return the amazing figures of 10-8-2-5. Shepherd's superb efforts allowed Glamorgan to celebrate a 115-run victory, and a month or so later, the Welsh side inflicted another heavy defeat on the luckless Leicestershire team, with Jeff Jones returning even more incredible figures than Shepherd's. This time the home side were bundled out for 40 on a green and lively Grace Road wicket as Jones recorded career best figures of 13-9-11-8.

Don Shepherd in action, vociferously appealing in Glamorgan's match against Essex at Swansea in 1969. The wicketkeeper is Eifion Jones and Peter Walker is the fielder in the leg-trap.

GLAMORGAN

	1ST INNINGS			2ND INNINGS		
A. Jones	c Hallam	b Savage	108	c Hallam	b Savage	8
A.R. Lewis		b Lock	1	c Inman	b Barratt	44
P.M. Walker	not out		79	c Inman	b Barratt	55
A.H.M. Rees	not out		1	not out		23
J.S. Pressdee				c van Geloven	b Lock	4
H.D.S. Miller				lbw	b Lock	1
E.J. Lewis				c Savage	b Barratt	1
D.J. Shepherd					b Barratt	2
+D.G.L. Evans				run out		0
I.J. Jones				c van Geloven	b Lock	6
*O.S.Wheatley						
Extras		(B 4, LB 3, W 4, NB 5)	16		(B 7, LB 1)	8
TOTAL		(for 2 wickets dec)	205		(for 9 wickets dec)	152

FOW: 1-15, 2-188

1-17, 2-98, 3-116, 4-117,5 -118
6-119, 7-129, 8-141, 9-152

Bowling	O	M	R	W	Bowling	O	M	R	W
van Geloven	19	6	45	0	van Geloven	8	3	14	0
Marner	9	2	30	0	Marner	4	1	11	0
Lock	20	1	58	1	Lock	15.3	1	56	3
Savage	21	9	41	1	Savage	7	0	25	1
Barratt	9	3	15	0	Barrett	12	2	38	4

LEICESTERSHIRE

	1ST INNINGS			2ND INNINGS		
*M.R. Hallam	not out		95	c A. Lewis	b Wheatley	6
B.J. Booth	lbw	b I.J. Jones	1		b I.J. Jones	3
J. Birkenshaw	c A. Jones	b Pressdee	11	c Evans	b E.J. Lewis	11
S. Jayasinghe		run out	2	c Evans	b Shepherd	5
C.C. Inman		b Rees	74	lbw	b Pressdee	2
P.T. Marner		not out	16	c I.J. Jones	b Shepherd	5
J. van Geloven				c Pressdee	b Shepherd	0
G.A.R. Lock					b Shepherd	1
+R. Julian					b E.J. Lewis	0
R.J. Barratt				not out		0
J.S. Savage				c Pressdee	b Shepherd	0
Extras		(B 4, LB 6)	10			0
TOTAL		(for 4 wickets dec)	209			33

FOW: 1-7, 2-31, 3-34, 4-170

1-7, 2-13, 3-17, 4-19, 5-21
6-32, 7-32, 8-33, 9-33

Bowling	O	M	R	W	Bowling	O	M	R	W
A.R. Lewis	2	0	10	0	I.J. Jones	4	1	12	1
I.J. Jones	12	6	18	1	Wheatley	3	1	5	1
Wheatley	10	5	19	0	Shepherd	10	8	2	5
Shepherd	19	9	36	0	E.J. Lewis	5	3	7	2
E.J. Lewis	12	4	35	0	Pressdee	4	1	7	1
Pressdee	13	3	30	1					
Miller	4	2	9	0					
A. Jones	4	2	13	0					
Rees	4.3	0	29	1					

Glamorgan won by 115 runs

YORKSHIRE

9, 10 July 1965 at Swansea

Glamorgan's match against Yorkshire at Swansea saw Glamorgan record a 31-run victory inside two days, with Glamorgan's two spin bowlers, Don Shepherd and Jim Pressdee, each taking nine wickets in an innings – Pressdee in the first, and Shepherd in the second. Their feat took place on a Swansea wicket which took spin from the outset, and in a match where the highest individual score of 46 came from Doug Padgett in Yorkshire's second innings as the Tykes chased a target on the dry and crumbly surface.

Aware that the wicket would turn, Wheatley batted first and only Alan Rees and Euros Lewis looked comfortable against the spin of Brian Close and Ray Illingworth. It was a great credit to the two Welshmen that Glamorgan made 140, as the Yorkshire batsmen were soon in deep trouble against the left-arm spin of Jim Pressdee. Three batsmen got into the 20s, but nobody, not even the mighty Geoff Boycott, stayed for any lengthy period.

The run out of Jack Hampshire halted the procession against Pressdee's bowling, and also stopped him from emulating Mercer's feat of taking ten wickets in an innings. Even so, Pressdee quickly mopped up the tail, and ended with career best figures of 9-43 as Glamorgan gained a valuable first innings lead of 44.

Yorkshire opened the attack with their spinners when Glamorgan batted again, and they had no need to call upon the services of fiery pace bowler Fred Trueman, as Ray Illingworth and Don Wilson made short work of Glamorgan's second innings. For the second time in the match, Euros Lewis offered doughty resistance, but wickets fell at the other end, as the Welsh county were reduced to 93-9.

Some 'old fashioned' tail-end slogging by Don Shepherd and Ossie Wheatley then tipped the balance back in Glamorgan's favour, adding 28 invaluable runs to set up an intriguing finale, with Yorkshire chasing 166 to win. Yorkshire seemed to have regained the initiative as Boycott and Padget shared a productive stand of 64 for the second wicket, but when Boycott was superbly caught by Peter Walker off Pressdee's bowling, it heralded a remarkable collapse against Shepherd's off-cutters.

Only Jack Hampshire, with 2 mighty sixes and 5 fours, offered anything more than token resistance against Shepherd's clever bowling. The experienced spinner took the final eight wickets in fairly quick succession, to finish with figures of 9-48 as Glamorgan completed another remarkable victory at their St Helen's ground.

Jim Pressdee

Don Shepherd

Glamorgan won the toss and elected to bat   *Umpires: C. Cook and C.G. Pepper*

GLAMORGAN   1ST INNINGS   2ND INNINGS

A. Jones	run out		19	cWilson	b Illingworth	7
B. Hedges		b Close	11	c Sharpe	b Wilson	28
A.R. Lewis	lbw	b Close	19	c Hampshire	b Wilson	20
A. Rees		b Illingworth	34	c Trueman	b Illingworth	0
J.S. Pressdee	lbw	b Illingworth	0	lbw	b Wilson	5
P.M. Walker		b Illingworth	1	c Taylor	b Wilson	0
E.J. Lewis	c and	b Close	30	not out		29
W.D. Slade	cTaylor	b Close	12		b Close	4
+D.G.L. Evans	not out		11		b Illingworth	1
D.J. Shepherd	c Boycott	b Close	0	c Sharpe	b Wilson	16
*O.S. Wheatley	cTaylor	b Close	1	c Hampshire	b Close	11
Extras		(LB 2)	2			
TOTAL			**140**			**121**

FOW: 1-17, 2-42, 3-71, 4-72, 5-74,   1-23, 2-28, 3-57, 4-58, 5-63,
6-107, 7-119, 8-130, 9-130   6-64, 7-69, 8-72, 9-93

Bowling	O	M	R	W	Bowling	O	M	R	W
Trueman	3	0	4	0	Close	10.3	3	25	2
Nicholson	5	3	2	0	Illingworth	24	5	59	3
Close	22.5	8	52	6	Wilson	13	3	37	5
Illingworth	24	6	68	3					
Wilson	4	2	12	0					

YORKSHIRE   1ST INNINGS   2ND INNINGS

G. Boycott	c A.R. Lewis	b Pressdee	18	c Walker	b Pressdee	21
K. Taylor	c Wheatley	b Pressdee	21		b Shepherd	4
D.E.V. Padgett	c Slade	b Pressdee	1	c Pressdee	b Shepherd	46
P.J. Sharpe	c Shepherd	b Pressdee	4		b Shepherd	9
*D.B. Close	c Shepherd	b Pressdee	23	lbw	b Shepherd	0
J.H. Hampshire	run out		4		b Shepherd	41
R. Illingworth	c Slade	b Pressdee	4	c Slade	b Shepherd	0
+J.G. Binks	c Wheatley	b Pressdee	20	lbw	b Shepherd	1
F.S. Trueman	c Evans	b Pressdee	0	c Rees	b Shepherd	0
D. Wilson	c E.J. Lewis	b Pressdee	0	st Evans	b Shepherd	8
A.G. Nicholson	not out		1	not out		0
Extras					(B 1, LB 3)	4
TOTAL			**96**			**134**

FOW: 1-31, 2-33, 3-37, 4-63, 5-68,   1-4, 2-68, 3-72, 4-72, 5-74,
6-73, 7-76, 8-84, 9-84   6-119, 7-119, 8-124, 9-129

Bowling	O	M	R	W	Bowling	O	M	R	W
Wheatley	2	0	6	0	Wheatley	4	1	3	0
Walker	2	0	14	0	Pressdee	26	8	73	1
Pressdee	23.3	12	43	9	Shepherd	27.5	12	48	9
Shepherd	23	12	33	0	E.J. Lewis	10	5	6	0

Glamorgan won by 31 runs

THE AUSTRALIANS

3, 4, 5 August 1968 at Swansea

August 1968 will always be remembered as the month when Garry Sobers created a new world record by hitting Malcolm Nash for 6 sixes in an over at Swansea in Glamorgan's Championship match with Nottinghamshire. However, the Welsh county's supporters prefer to recall the month as the time when Glamorgan recorded a famous double over the touring Australians.

Their defeat of the 1968 Australians saw intriguing parallels with their victory in 1964, as Glamorgan were unable to select a full strength eleven and, on the eve of the game, they lost their captain, Tony Lewis, with a throat infection. However, he had a wonderful deputy in Don Shepherd, and the acting Glamorgan leader struck the first blow by winning the toss on a typical Swansea wicket – dry, easy paced and one which was likely to assist the spin bowlers later in the game.

Alan Jones was in scintillating form and together with new signing, Majid Khan of Pakistan, they delighted the capacity crowd with some majestic strokeplay. Majid hit an effortless half-century in just 45 minutes with 3 sixes and 7 fours, whilst Alan Jones used his feet time and again, dancing down the wicket to pierce the field with some exquisitely timed strokes. He was on the verge of becoming only the second Glamorgan centurion against Australia when, on 99, he lofted Ashley Mallett high over mid-on, but straight into the hands on Neil Hawke on the boundary ropes.

Mallett and Gleeson soon polished off the rest of the Glamorgan batting, and as tea was taken during the change of innings, the minds of many of the players and spectators went back to Australia's visit to Swansea in 1964 when the tourists had a dramatic collapse after tea. Surely it couldn't happen again, but sure enough in the 'Celtic cauldron' that is St Helen's, the Australians slumped once again to 77-6 by the close, falling to the controlled left-arm swing of uncapped bowler Malcolm Nash, and the off-breaks of another reserve bowler, Brian Lewis. Indeed, the events after tea were an almost copybook repeat of their encounter four years before, as the Australians were harried and pressurised into making mistakes, whilst the athletic Glamorgan

Left: Catches win matches – Roger Davis brilliantly catches John Gleeson. Right: Bryan Davis

Alan Jones in action.

fielders pulled off some fine catches.

The Australian resistance ended on the second morning, thanks to some smart wicketkeeping from Eifion Jones, and further deft fielding close to the wicket. With a first innings lead of 114, Don Shepherd told his batsmen to go for quick runs in the second innings, knowing full well that it would be imperative for Glamorgan to have plenty of time in which to try and bowl out the Australians for a second time.

Roger Davis, assisted by his West Indian namesake, Bryan, responded perfectly. Their rousing second wicket stand of 100, made in a fraction under an hour, helped to consolidate Glamorgan's position. The West Indian was particularly fierce on the Australian bowlers, hitting a six and 11 fours in his hour long stay at the crease. Alan Rees, Tony Cordle and Shepherd himself also weighed in with some hefty blows later in the afternoon, and the acting captain was able to declare at the close, leaving Australia the whole of the final day to chase 365.

The third day dawned dry and sunny and, from an early hour, the Swansea ground was full of excited chatter about another famous Welsh sporting victory. Once again, the Glamorgan fielders rose to the occasion, with Alan Rees swooping at cover point to run out Ian Redpath, and soon afterwards Malcolm Nash produced a fine 'nip-backer' to bowl John Inverarity.

However, Paul Sheahan and Bob Cowper easily settled in against Nash and Cordle, and they found runs easy to come by against the two young seamers. Shepherd decided to make a change, bringing on himself and Brian Lewis in an attempt to stifle the Australian progress. The scoring rate duly dropped and Cowper eventually perished, swinging across the line against Lewis to give Eifion Jones an easy catch.

Les Joslin soon fell to Lewis, so captain Barry Jarman came in with the specific intention of hitting the spinners off their length. He made a few firm blows, before being deceived by Shepherd's clever flight, and he was well caught at short-leg by Roger Davis. The Welsh fielders continued to excel and Majid ran out Mallett, as Sheahan attempted to scamper a single to bring up his century, whilst Roger Davis clung superbly onto a thick edge from Gleeson to leave Australia reeling at 219-8.

The only man standing between Glamorgan and another victory was Paul Sheahan, and after reaching his century, he showed his fighting resolve by hoisting the Welsh spinners high into the members' enclosure. On 120 he survived a sharp chance to Brian Lewis but, a few overs later, he struck a sizzling drive straight back to the bowler, Peter Walker, and Walker made no mistake in holding onto the catch.

Alan Connolly and Dave Renneburg were equally determined to go down fighting, and both tailenders made some hearty blows before Renneburg miscued another expansive stroke against Walker and was well caught by Majid at cover. The ecstatic crowd needed no invitation to show their delight, and they quickly swarmed onto the St Helen's pitch to celebrate Glamorgan's feat in becoming the first county to defeat Australia on consecutive tours.

As the jubilant supporters gathered below the players' balcony, Welsh songs soon filled the air, and there was even a rendition of *Waltzing Matilda*. A hush then descended as Don Shepherd and Barry Jarman addressed the crowd. Sustained applause greeted Don Shepherd in recognition of his astute and shrewd captaincy, and when Jarman spoke to the throng, he was full of praise for Glamorgan's efforts, and finished by wryly saying 'What's new about being beaten by Glamorgan!'

Barry Jarman tells the crowd after Glamorgan's famous victory: 'What's new about being beaten by Glamorgan?' – much to the delight of their acting captain Don Shepherd.

Glamorgan won the toss and elected to bat   *Umpires: J.F. Crapp and C.G. Pepper*

GLAMORGAN

		1ST INNINGS			2ND INNINGS	
A. Jones	c Hawke	b Mallett	99	c Sheahan	b Mallett	10
R.C. Davis		b Connolly	24	c Gleeson	b Hawke	59
B.A. Davis	c Cowper	b Gleeson	1	c and	b Cowper	66
P..M. Walker	c Inverarity	b Cowper	19	lbw	b Gleeson	13
Majid Khan	st Jarman	b Mallett	55	c Sheahan	b Hawke	13
A.H.M. Rees	c Inverarity	b Gleeson	0	not out		33
+E.W. Jones	c Sheahan	b Mallett	3			
M.A. Nash	c Inverarity	b Mallett	0	(7) c Cowper	b Gleeson	7
A.E. Cordle	st Jarman	b Gleeson	1	(8) c Redpath	b Gleeson	17
B. Lewis	not out		6	(9) st Jarman	b Gleeson	4
*D.J. Shepherd	c Redpath	b Gleeson	10	(10)c Connolly	b Mallett	14
Extras		(B 2, LB 3, W 0, NB 1)	6		(B 2, LB 10, NB 2)	14
TOTAL			**224**		(for 9 wkts dec)	**250**

FOW: 1-50, 2-51, 3-110, 4-194, 5-203,   1-15, 2-115, 3-148, 4-157, 5-165,
       6-203, 7-204, 8-207, 9-211   6-193, 7-209, 8-227, 9-250

Bowling	O	M	R	W		O	M	R	W
Renneberg	11	2	35	0	Renneberg	8	2	25	0
Hawke	3	0	10	0	Hawke	14	4	27	2
Connolly	14	4	21	1	Connolly	5	0	17	0
Gleeson	23.3	9	73	4	Gleeson	17	3	56	4
Mallett	12	3	46	4	Mallett	16.2	1	85	2
Cowper	9	2	33	1	Cowper	8	0	26	1

AUSTRALIANS

		1ST INNINGS			2ND INNINGS	
R.J. Inverarity	c R.Davis	b Lewis	31		b Nash	28
*+B.N. Jarman		run out	1	c R. Davis	b Shepherd	13
I.R. Redpath		b Nash	13	run out		13
R.M. Cowper	c Walker	b Nash	0	c E. Jones	b Lewis	42
A.P. Sheahan		b Lewis	12	c and	b Walker	137
L.R. Joslin	c Majid Khan	b Lewis	19	c and	b Lewis	7
N.J.N. Hawke	c and	b Lewis	6	c Majid Khan	b Shepherd	6
A.A. Mallett	c E. Jones	b Nash	11	run out		4
J.W. Gleeson	c E. Jones	b Nash	11	c R. Davis	b Lewis	0
A.N. Connolly	lbw	b Nash	1	not out		22
D.A. Renneberg	not out		0	c Majid Khan	b Walker	3
Extras		(LB 3, NB 2)	5		(LB 10)	10
TOTAL			**110**			**285**

FOW: 1-3, 2-20, 3-22, 4-36, 5-77,   1-35, 2-45, 3-116, 4-128, 5-173,
       6-80, 7-91, 8-105, 9-109   6-195, 7-196, 8-219, 9-259

Bowling	O	M	R	W		O	M	R	W
Nash	15.3	6	28	5	Nash	10	2	22	1
Cordle	3	2	1	0	Cordle	8	1	34	0
Shepherd	16	9	11	0	Shepherd	27	9	63	2
Lewis	20	6	51	4	Lewis	32	4	131	3
Walker	8	3	14	0	Walker	8.2	2	25	2

Glamorgan won by 79 runs

Essex

30 August, 1, 2 September 1969 at Swansea

Wales had a momentous year in 1969 – Prince Charles, now the Patron of Glamorgan CCC was invested as Prince of Wales and, on the rugby field, the Welsh national side had another fine season. It was almost 'The Year of the Welsh' as Glamorgan won the County Championship in 1969, and in so doing became the first county side since Lancashire in 1930 to win the title without being beaten. Under the shrewd captaincy of Tony Lewis, Glamorgan registered eleven victories and this next pair of classic matches recall perhaps the two most important games from that wonderful summer.

This first classic game from the summer of '69 recalls what was the side's tenth, and most exciting victory of the season, against Essex over the August Bank Holiday period. Glamorgan had a game in hand over Gloucestershire, their nearest rivals, and knew that victory in two of their last three games would be sufficient to secure the Championship pennant. Home advantage for the match with Essex proved vital, and another massive crowd turned up to watch an enthralling game. Essex secured a lead on first innings by 95 runs, thanks to a sparkling century from Lee Irvine and a jaunty 70 from Essex captain and wicketkeeper Brian Taylor. When Glamorgan batted again, John Lever and Stuart Turner sent back Roger Davis, Majid Khan and Tony Lewis to leave the Welsh side on 123-4 at the close on the second day, just 28 runs ahead.

One of the key elements in Glamorgan's success during 1969 was their team spirit, and this was clearly evident on the final morning as first Alan Jones, and then Peter Walker, stubbornly fought back as the initiative swung in Glamorgan's favour. Malcolm Nash, Eifion Jones and Tony Cordle all chipped in with little cameos with the bat, allowing Tony Lewis to set Essex a fair target of 190 in two hours. Ossie Wheatley proceeded to made important inroads with the new ball as Essex slipped to 43-3, but Gordon Barker and Keith Fletcher then steadied the ship with a fighting stand for the fourth wicket. Spinners Don Shepherd and Roger Davis both conceded runs, but Tony Lewis had faith in his spin attack, and he kept them both on, knowing that something would happen sooner rather than later. And so it proved, as Davis lured Barker down the track to be stumped by Eifion Jones, before Fletcher was caught by Bryan Davis. Further wickets fell as Essex continued their run chase, and a breezy partnership between Robin Hobbs and Ray East took Essex agonisingly closer to the target. After a few near misses, Don Shepherd finally dismissed Hobbs in the penultimate over, and last man John Lever came in with Essex needing 8 runs and Glamorgan one more wicket. Amidst great tension, Lever and East furtively scampered singles and with three needed off the last ball, East deftly cut the ball down to the vacant third man boundary. For a heart-stopping moment, it looked like being a match winning stroke, but Wheatley ran around the ropes and sent an arrow-like throw over the top of the stumps. Eifion Jones did not have to move an inch, and he ran out Lever to leave Glamorgan the victors by one run.

Eifion Jones runs out John Lever to win the game for Glamorgan.

Glamorgan won the toss and elected to bat   *Umpires: D.J. Constant and G.H. Pope*

GLAMORGAN

1ST INNINGS				2ND INNINGS		
A. Jones	c Boyce	b Turner	75	c Taylor	b Lever	69
R.C. Davis	lbw	b Boyce	2		b Lever	2
Majid Khan	c Turner	b East	23		b Turner	28
*A.R. Lewis	c Taylor	b Turner	1	c Irvine	b Lever	21
B.A. Davis	c Ward	b East	78	c Irvine	b Hobbs	5
M.A. Nash	c Edmeades	b Lever	14		not out	36
P.M. Walker	c Barker	b Hobbs	14	c Ward	b Boyce	50
+E.W. Jones	c Fletcher	b East	0	st Taylor	b Hobbs	28
A.E. Cordle	c Taylor	b Boyce	20		b Hobbs	30
D.J. Shepherd	not out		2		not out	2
O.S. Wheatley	c and	b Hobbs	0			
Extras		(B 4, LB 3, NB 5)	12		(B 8, LB 2, NB 3)	13
TOTAL			**241**		(for 8 wkts dec)	**284**

FOW: 1-5, 2-58, 3-65, 4-156, 5-196
6-210, 7-210, 8-230, 9-239

1-8, 2-50, 3-90, 4-109, 5-144,
6-181, 7-227, 8-272

Bowling	O	M	R	W	Bowling	O	M	R	W
Boyce	18	3	52	2	Boyce	25	5	79	1
Lever	15	5	38	1	Lever	22	4	64	3
East	19	3	63	3	East	9	3	19	0
Turner	20	8	44	2	Turner	11	1	31	1
Hobbs	11.1	2	32	2	Hobbs	36	16	78	3
Fletcher	1	1	0	0					

ESSEX

1ST INNINGS				2ND INNINGS		
B. Ward	c R.Davis	b Wheatley	31	c R. Davis	b Wheatley	21
B.E.A. Edmeades	lbw	b Nash	4	c Lewis	b Wheatley	10
G. Barker	lbw	b Wheatley	17	st E. Jones	b R. Davis	28
K.W.R. Fletcher	lbw	b Wheatley	49	c B. Davis	b R. Davis	44
B.L. Irvine		b R. Davis	109		b Shepherd	29
K.D. Boyce	c B. Davis	b Shepherd	16	c Lewis	b R. Davis	11
*+ B. Taylor	c Cordle	b R. Davis	70	c Lewis	b Wheatley	5
S. Turner	not out		23	c R. Davis	b Shepherd	2
R.N.S. Hobbs	not out		8	c E. Jones	b Shepherd	17
R.E. East				not out		14
J.K. Lever				run out		2
Extras		(B 1, LB 7, NB 1)	9		(B 4, LB 1)	5
TOTAL		(for 7 wkts dec)	**336**			**188**

FOW: 1-5, 2-48, 3-63, 4-139, 5-165
6-294, 7-304

1-29, 2-36, 3-43, 4-109, 5-123,
6-125, 7-131, 8-163, 9-185

Bowling	O	M	R	W	Bowling	O	M	R	W
Nash	24	5	84	1	Nash	3	0	16	0
Wheatley	26	3	77	3	Wheatley	10	0	40	3
Cordle	8	2	32	0	Cordle	4	0	33	0
Shepherd	28	10	78	1	Shepherd	11	0	56	3
Walker	3	0	20	0	R. Davis	9	0	38	3
R. Davis	10	1	36	2					

Glamorgan won by 1 run

WORCESTERSHIRE

3, 4, 5 September 1969 at Cardiff

The nerve-jangling win over Essex meant that the Championship would be Glamorgan's if they defeated either Worcestershire or Surrey in their two remaining games. A crowd of over 10,000 flocked into the county's relatively new ground in Cardiff at Sophia Gardens, eager to witness the final chapter of a fantastic summer's events.

They were also fortunate to witness one of the greatest ever innings played in Glamorgan's history, as Majid Khan made a quite superb 156 out of 265 on a spiteful wicket. There had been concerns for the past three summers about the unpredictable nature of the surface at Sophia Gardens and the uneven way in which balls behaved on the wickets. Indeed, the Glamorgan batsmen were often quite upset not to be still playing on the benign surfaces at the Arms Park, which was being redeveloped as part of the Welsh Rugby Union's National Stadium.

Whilst there were doubts in the minds of some batsmen, Majid Khan remained unruffled and his almost magical batting completely mastered a useful Worcestershire attack. His graceful strokeplay resulted in sixteen elegantly struck boundaries, and although wickets fell regularly at the other end, the Pakistani always looked in complete control, with plenty of time to play even the most wicked of deliveries. When Worcestershire batted, they could only muster 183, with just Ron Headley and captain Tom Graveney looking at ease against Glamorgan's lively seam attack of Malcolm Nash and Ossie Wheatley, augmented by the off-cutters of Don Shepherd. Glamorgan extended their healthy lead in their second innings, thanks to an aggressive innings of 63 from Peter Walker, plus a breezy 39 from Eifion Jones, before the brave wicketkeeper was hit on the head by a short ball from Vanburn Holder. Jones was helped into the dressing room feeling quite groggy, and when Tony Lewis declared, setting the visitors a target of 255, it was Majid Khan who deputised for a while behind the stumps. But the doughty gloveman was not going to miss out on the kill, and despite still feeling giddy, he went back onto the field.

By this time, Tony Cordle had got in amongst the wickets, sending back Rodney Cass, Alan Ormrod, Basil d'Oliveira and Tom Graveney with just 66 runs on the board. With Eifion Jones back behind the stumps, Tony Lewis brought Don Shepherd into the attack, and with a broad beam on the veteran's face, he quickly stifled any thoughts Worcestershire had of mounting a recovery, and proceeded to work his way through the rest of their batting. As the curtain came down on a fine summer, it was fitting that Don Shepherd should take the 2,000th wicket of his career during Worcestershire's second innings. Indeed, it was the old warhorse who ended the game by having Brian Brain caught off bat and box in the slips by Bryan Davis, to give Glamorgan victory by 147 runs, and the county title for the second time in their history.

Part of the back page of the Western Mail for 6 September 1969, showing the fans engulfing the players as they left the field.

Glamorgan won the toss and elected to bat   *Umpires: G.H. Pope and H. Yarnold*

GLAMORGAN   1ST INNINGS

				2ND INNINGS			
A. Jones		b Gifford	37	lbw		b Brain	7
R.C. Davis	retired hurt		2				
Majid Khan	c Headley	b Gifford	156 (2)	c Graveney		b Gifford	34
*A.R. Lewis	c Holder	b Gifford	0 (3)	c Graveney		b Brain	0
B.A. Davis	c Holder	b Gifford	9 (4)	c Headley		b Holder	16
P.M. Walker	c and	b Slade	27 (5)	not out			63
+E.W. Jones	c Ormrod	b Gifford	16 (6)	retired hurt			39
M.A. Nash		b Gifford	6 (7)	not out			9
A.E. Cordle	c Headley	b Gifford	2 (8)			b Brain	0
D.J. Shepherd	c and	b Slade	3				
O.S. Wheatley	not out		2				
Extras		(LB 2, NB 3)	5		(LB 2, W 1, NB 2)		5
TOTAL			**265**	(for 5 wkts dec)			**173**

FOW: 1-110, 2-118, 3-179, 4-221, 5-250,   1-20, 2-31, 3-32, 4-76, 5-144
6-258, 7-258, 8-262, 9-265

Bowling	O	M	R	W	Bowler	O	M	R	W
Holder	7	1	29	0	Holder	22	5	59	1
Brain	8	1	30	0	Brain	23	6	64	3
Gifford	36	7	99	7	Gifford	9	1	27	1
Standen	3	1	13	0	Slade	8	2	18	0
Slade	30.2	5	83	2					
D'Oliveira	1	0	6	0					

WORCESTERSHIRE 1ST INNINGS

				2ND INNINGS			
R.G.A. Headley	c Lewis	b Shepherd	71	c B. Davis		b Nash	7
+G.R. Cass	c E.W.Jones	b Wheatley	0	c and		b Cordle	30
J.A. Ormrod	c Walker	b Wheatley	0	c Nash		b Cordle	5
B.L. D'Oliveira	c sub	b Nash	3	lbw		b Cordle	17
*T.W. Graveney	lbw	b Walker	43	c sub		b Cordle	19
T.J. Yardley	c Walker	b Shepherd	8	c B. Davis		b Shepherd	1
D.N. Slade	c Majid	b Shepherd	7	c Majid		b Shepherd	3
J.A. Standen		b Nash	21	c Majid		b Cordle	5
N. Gifford	c Majid	b Nash	1			b Shepherd	1
V.A. Holder	lbw	b Nash	14	not out			5
B.M. Brain	not out		4	c B. Davis		b Shepherd	9
Extras		(B 4, LB 4, NB 3)	11		(B 2, LB 3, NB 1)		6
TOTAL			**183**				**108**

FOW: 1-0, 2-0, 3-14, 4-81, 5-97,   1-20, 2-36, 3-60, 4-63, 5-66
6-139, 7-142, 8-143, 9-168   6-70, 7-81, 8-94, 9-98

Bowling	O	M	R	W	Bowling	O	M	R	W
Nash	17	4	43	4	Nash	6	1	24	1
Wheatley	22	10	20	2	Wheatley	10	4	16	0
Walker	24	12	34	1	Shepherd	11.5	4	20	4
Shepherd	34	13	69	3	Cordle	15	2	42	5
Cordle	6	4	6	0					

Glamorgan won by 147 runs

SOMERSET

5 September 1976 at Cardiff

Glamorgan had had a rotten season in 1976, so when Somerset travelled to Cardiff for the final match of the Sunday League season it looked a formality that they would secure the win they needed to give the West Country side their first title. Little had gone right for the Welsh county during the long, hot summer of 1976. Captain Majid Khan had quit in mid-season, and several other players had departed, muttering gloomily about dressing room strife and a rift between the players and the committee.

It looked as if another embarrassing episode was about to take place on the morning of this classic match, as the Glamorgan stewards and gatemen arrived at Sophia Gardens to find the ground already almost full of Somerset supporters. Events on the field, however, soon gave Glamorgan more to smile about as in the early overs Brian Close, the stalwart Somerset skipper, dropped Alan Jones at square leg.

This proved to be a costly miss as the Glamorgan captain went on to top score with 70 and, with a few hefty blows from Malcolm Nash, Glamorgan were able to set Somerset a target of 192 in 39 overs. The visitors got off to a quite shaky start, losing Peter Denning, Brian Close and Ian Botham all to the left-arm swing of Nash. Brian Rose and Merv Kitchen then steadied the Somerset innings with a partnership of 70 for the fourth wicket, before Graham Burgess and Dennis Breakwell continued their good work.

As Somerset moved closer to their target, Alan Jones brought Nash back into the attack for his final three overs. With the score on 171, he bowled Breakwell and eight runs later Derek Taylor was run out as the nerve ends started to jangle. A further eight runs had been added as Nash bowled the final over of the game, and in the mounting tension, the pressure seemed to be getting to the Somerset batsmen as another mix-up occurred and Keith Jennings was run out.

Graham Burgess was still there, however, and he faced the final ball from Nash with Somerset needing three runs to tie the game and secure the Sunday League trophy. Burgess boldly hit the ball back over Nash's head down to the sightscreen at the Cathedral Road end of the ground. The Somerset supporters started to cheer, believing that Burgess had hit the winning runs, but Alan Jones calmly ran in from the boundary and threw the ball back to Nash as Burgess and Colin Dredge completed their second run. They had to get a third run to win the trophy, so they set off in desperation as Nash lobbed the ball gently back to Eifion Jones, who then removed the bails with Dredge well short of his ground, and Somerset one run short of their target.

Alan Jones

Malcolm Nash

GLAMORGAN INNINGS

*A. Jones		b Dredge	70
G.P. Ellis	c Taylor	b Botham	12
D.A. Francis		b Jennings	36
M.A. Nash		b Moseley	43
J.A. Hopkins	run out		7
A.E. Cordle	c Rose	b Botham	9
+E.W. Jones	run out		0
G. Richards	not out		0
A.H. Wilkins			
B.J. Lloyd			
D.L. Williams			
Extras		(B 12, LB 1, NB 1)	14
TOTAL		(for 7 wickets)	**191**

FOW:1-31, 2-123, 3-134, 4-145, 5-180, 6-189, 7-190

Bowling	O	M	R	W
Moseley	8	0	31	1
Botham	7	0	41	2
Burgess	8	0	32	0
Jennings	8	0	39	1
Dredge	8	0	34	1

SOMERSET INNINGS

B.C. Rose	c E. Jones	b Williams	39
P.W. Denning	lbw	b Nash	6
*D.B. Close	c Wilkins	b Nash	1
I.T. Botham	c and	b Nash	9
M.J. Kitchen		b Wilkins	46
G.I. Burgess	not out		48
D. Breakwell		b Nash	21
+D.J.S. Taylor	run out		8
K.V. Jennings	run out		1
C.H. Dredge	run out		0
H.R. Moseley			
Extras		(LB 10, NB 1)	11
TOTAL		(for 9 wickets)	**190**

FOW: 1-11, 2-15, 3-27, 4-97, 5-127, 6-171, 7-180, 8-188, 9-190

Bowling	O	M	R	W
Nash	8	1	35	4
Cordle	8	1	38	0
Ellis	8	0	34	0
Lloyd	4	0	17	0
Williams	7	0	32	1
Wilkins	4	0	23	1

Glamorgan won by 1 run

LEICESTERSHIRE
17, 18, 19 August 1977 at Swansea

Glamorgan had tasted little success in one-day cricket, so it was no surprise at the start of the 1977 season to see them listed as rank outsiders for the Gillette Cup, the premier limited-overs competition. However, the Welsh county made a complete mockery of these odds, put together a series of comprehensive victories and reached the Lord's final of a one day competition for the first time in their history. Glamorgan's progress in the 1977 Gillette Cup began with a bye in the first round, before in mid-July defeating Worcestershire at New Road by four wickets. Young batsmen Arthur Francis and Mike Llewellyn both scored half-centuries as Glamorgan recorded their first win in the competition for the small matter of five years! The Welsh side were then quite fortunate to secure a home draw for the quarter-final, against Surrey at Sophia Gardens. It was a contest which drew a capacity crowd to the Cardiff ground, and it proved to be a good day all round for the club, as gate receipts exceeded £6,500 and Surrey were defeated by four wickets. This time it was the turn of captain Alan Jones and new overseas signing Collis King to score half-centuries as Glamorgan successfully chased a target of 200.

Lady luck was on Glamorgan's side once again with the draw for the semi-finals, giving Alan Jones' side a home tie against Leicestershire at Swansea. Persistent rain intervened to force the match over three days, but after an entire washout on the first day, Glamorgan won a vital toss on the second day and, with the outfield still damp, Alan Jones invited Leicestershire to bat first.

The loss of early wickets and further interruptions by rain hampered the visitors. Although David Gower and Brian Davison took the total to 87, their dismissal in successive overs dealt Leicestershire a blow from which they never fully recovered. Alan Wilkins and Gwyn Richards both bowled accurate spells and, with the aid of some razor-sharp ground fielding, they restricted Leicestershire to a modest 172-7. Alan Jones and John Hopkins launched the Glamorgan innings in a commanding way, adding 108 for the first wicket in almost even time before both were out, and a slight stutter took place against Leicestershire's experienced spin attack of John Steele, Ray Illingworth and Jack Birkenshaw. In the space of ten overs, Glamorgan added just 11 runs, but lost two further wickets. Matters were made worse when Mike Llewellyn was run out, leaving Glamorgan on 147-5 with Gwyn Richards as the last specialist batsman at the crease. But the youngster had the support of Eifion Jones, the county's vastly experienced wicketkeeper, and the Leicestershire spinners were coming towards the end of their twelve over allocations.

Richards and Jones kept their nerve and carefully added the 28 runs Glamorgan needed. When the target was reduced to single figures, a chorus *of Mae Hen Wlad Fy Nhadau* drifted out from the packed pavilion and there was an enormous cheer as the winning runs were hit with 15 balls to go, giving Glamorgan a place at a Lord's final for the first time in their history.

Brian Davison hits a boundary watched by wicketkeeper Eifion Jones. The slip fielders are Collis King and John Hopkins, whilst the non-striker is David Gower.

LEICESTERSHIRE INNINGS

J.F. Steele	c E.W. Jones	b Nash	1
D.I. Gower	c Wilkins	b Richards	43
J.C. Balderstone	lbw	b Cordle	11
B.F. Davison	lbw	b Wilkins	40
+ R.W. Tolchard	run out		2
J. Birkenshaw	c Hopkins	b Wilkins	5
N.M. McVicker	c and	b Richards	4
*R. Illingworth	not out		22
P. Booth	not out		40
A. Ward			
K. Higgs			
Extras		(LB 4)	4
TOTAL		(for 7 wickets)	**172**

FOW: 1-1, 2-26, 3-87, 4-97, 5-98, 6-104, 7-109

Bowling	O	M	R	W
Nash	12	4	38	1
Cordle	7	2	21	1
Cartwright	11	1	34	0
King	6	1	24	0
Richards	12	4	17	2
Wilkins	12	5	34	2

GLAMORGAN INNINGS

*A. Jones	c Steele	b Birkenshaw	38
J.A. Hopkins		b Birkenshaw	63
R.C. Ontong	st Tolchard	b Balderstone	14
C.L. King	c McVicker	b Illingworth	1
M.J. Llewellyn	run out		14
G. Richards	not out		17
+E.W. Jones	not out		14
Extras		(B 10, LB 3, NB 1)	14
TOTAL		(for 5 wickets)	**175**

DNB: M.A. Nash, A.E. Cordle, T.W. Cartwright, A.H. Wilkins
FOW: 1-108, 2-109, 3-118, 4-136, 5-147

Bowling	O	M	R	W
Higgs	7	1	19	0
Ward	2	1	7	0
Booth	6.3	1	22	0
Steele	12	2	30	0
Illingworth	12	2	40	1
Birkenshaw	12	7	21	2
Balderstone	6	2	22	1

Glamorgan won by 5 wickets

MIDDLESEX

3 September 1977 at Lord's

The victory over Leicestershire in the semi-final at Swansea led to delirious celebrations at the St Helen's ground. The sound of singing and champagne corks popping must have sounded like a dream to Glamorgan's young professionals, who had so far experienced the less glamorous side to professional cricket. Rodney Ontong was one of these, and he later recalled how 'it was an unbelievable feeling, sitting in the dressing room. Taking it all in, whilst the crowd carried on singing outside. We didn't even know who we were going to be playing at Lord's for a week, as Middlesex spent six days struggling against Somerset. But to be quite honest, we were not really interested in who our opponents were going to be – we would have played anyone!'

On 26 August, Middlesex eventually defeated Somerset at Lord's and they were confirmed as Glamorgan's opponents in the final. Over the next three weeks, South Wales was gripped by cricket fever, as in almost every pub and club there was excited chatter about the final. Ticket applications were made and travel plans were finalised, and the net result was that Lord's, on the morning of the final, was alive with Welsh voices, after an exodus across the Severn Estuary by train, coach and car.

Lord's seemed more like Cardiff Arms Park on the day of a rugby international, especially as the weather was distinctly autumnal, with overcast skies. The pitch was only just fit for play after torrential overnight rain, so the toss was clearly going to be crucial. On this occasion, lady luck deserted Alan Jones, as Mike Brearley won the toss and had little hesitation in inviting Glamorgan to bat. But it was not all doom and gloom for the Welsh side, as the slow wicket and damp run-ups restricted Middlesex's West Indian paceman Wayne Daniel. However, Mike Selvey bowled accurately at the other end and his tight bowling, together with the wet outfield, restricted Alan Jones and John Hopkins. Jones eventually fell to Selvey trying to force the pace, and the England seamer then claimed the prized wicket of Collis King for 8, before Mike Gatting had Rodney Ontong caught behind for a duck.

Glamorgan had slumped to 50-3, before John Hopkins and Mike Llewellyn gave the innings a much needed impetus. Llewellyn was in particularly aggressive form, and his first three scoring

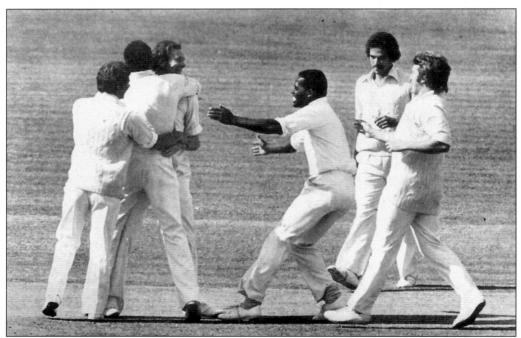

The Glamorgan players congratulate Malcolm Nash after his first ball dismissal of Mike Brearley.

Man of the match Clive Radley with the Gillette Cup.

strokes were four, six and four, off Gatting, before striking an enormous six from Emburey high over long on and into the guttering on the roof of the BBC commentary box, on the top tier of the famous pavilion.

Llewellyn was eventually dismissed for 62 by Norman Featherstone, and after his removal, the innings rather fell away in the closing overs, as Featherstone cheaply claimed the wickets of Malcolm Nash and Tom Cartwright. With the Middlesex side brimful of class batsmen, it was imperative that Glamorgan took early wickets. In Malcolm Nash, Glamorgan had one of the finest new ball bowlers in the country, and the left-armer produced a peach of a delivery with the very first ball of the innings. The ball drifted across the bat of opener Mike Brearley, took the edge, and he was caught behind by Eifion Jones. The voices of hundreds of hearty Welshmen rang out to the strains of the Welsh National Anthem as Brearley quietly walked off, and in the next over it looked as if the Welsh supporters would have more to sing about as Clive Radley edged a ball from Nash straight to second slip. But Collis King spilled the chance in what proved to be the pivotal moment in this classic match.

Radley was typically unflappable, and he quietly got his head down in resolute fashion, and worked the ball around, and into the gaps for ones and twos. As the shine went off the ball, the Glamorgan bowlers found less and less assistance. Collis King partially atoned for his costly mistake by having Gatting caught by John Hopkins, whilst Graham Barlow was trapped leg before by Gwyn Richards. But Radley was in complete control at the other end, and he calmly guided Middlesex to a comfortable five-wicket win.

Alan Jones gives a post-match interview to former Glamorgan player Peter Walker, now a BBC commentator.

Some of the happy band of Glamorgan spectators in front of the Lord's pavilion.

Middlesex won the toss and elected to field   Umpires: D.J. Constant and T.W. Spencer

GLAMORGAN INNINGS

*A. Jones	lbw	b Selvey	18
J.A. Hopkins		b Edmonds	47
C.L. King	c Barlow	b Selvey	8
R.C. Ontong	c Gould	b Gatting	0
M.J. Llewellyn	c Gatting	b Featherstone	62
G. Richards		b Edmonds	3
+E.W. Jones	run out		11
M.A. Nash	c Gatting	b Featherstone	3
A.E. Cordle	not out		8
T.W. Cartwright	st Gould	b Featherstone	3
A.H. Wilkins			
Extras		(B 7, LB 5, W 2)	14
TOTAL		(for 9 wkts)	**177**

FOW: 1-21, 2-47, 3-50, 4-115, 5-129,
6-163, 7-163, 8-171, 9-177

Bowling	O	M	R	W
Daniel	11	0	41	0
Selvey	12	4	22	2
Gatting	7	1	28	1
Edmonds	12	3	23	2
Emburey	12	2	32	0
Featherstone	6	0	17	3

MIDDLESEX INNINGS

*J.M. Brearley	c E.Jones	b Nash	0
M.J. Smith	lbw	b Cartwright	22
C.T. Radley	not out		85
M.W. Gatting	c Hopkins	b King	15
G.D. Barlow	lbw	b Richards	27
N.G. Featherstone		b Nash	3
P.H. Edmonds	not out		9
Extras		(B 6, LB 11)	17
TOTAL		(for 5 wkts)	**178**

DNB: +I.J. Gould, J.E. Emburey, M.W.W. Selvey, W.W. Daniel
FOW: 1-0, 2-45, 3-72, 4-146, 5-153

Bowling	O	M	R	W
Nash	12	3	31	2
Cordle	8.4	1	29	0
Cartwright	12	2	32	1
King	5	1	19	1
Richards	12	2	23	1
Wilkins	6	0	27	0

Middlesex won by 5 wickets

SUSSEX
23 July 1978 at Hastings

The Sunday League contest between Sussex and Glamorgan at Hastings in 1978 was a one-day game with everything – runs, wickets, fine catches, accurate bowling and the outcome remaining in the balance until the penultimate ball. However, if there were any budding poets in the crowd that afternoon, I doubt if they would have written about 'a breathless hush in the close tonight', as during the second half of this classic match, proceedings had to be temporarily halted as the Red Arrows aerobatics team, performing at a nearby air show, repeatedly flew low over the ground with a deafening roar.

Earlier in the afternoon, Alan Jones had won the toss and invited Sussex to bat first in this match screened live on BBC 2 as part of their *Sunday Cricket* programme. Kepler Wessels and Gehan Mendis launched the innings with a brisk opening partnership, before Imran Khan hit a forceful 54, during the course of which he hit 7 fours, plus a huge six off Peter Swart. He eventually fell attempting a repeat of the shot, only to be magnificently caught at long on by a diving Barry Lloyd. Imran's departure led to a drop in the scoring rate as Glamorgan's young spin bowlers, Gwyn Richards and Barry Lloyd, put a brake on the run scoring as Sussex ended on 188-7.

Alan Jones and John Hopkins made a rapid start to the Glamorgan innings, but their progress was halted several times by the din of the Red Arrows swooping over the ground at rooftop height. After the openers had departed, Rodney Ontong and Malcolm Nash increased the tempo with further lusty blows, but Glamorgan's progress was stifled by some fine fielding – firstly, Imran took a splendid running catch to dismiss Nash, and then Arthur Francis was run out attempting a suicidal run. Eifion Jones remained unflappable at the other end, even when the game went into the final over with Glamorgan still needing 13. Facing the experienced Geoff Arnold, Barry Lloyd got a thick edge to the first ball that flew to the boundary for four. After blocking the next delivery, Lloyd hit two more valuable runs, before scampering a single to leave Eifion Jones needing to hit six runs off the final two balls.

The doughty wicketkeeper only needed one ball, as he swung the fifth delivery of the over high over square leg for six. It stunned the large crowd of holidaymakers, but as Jones explained afterwards, it was a pre-planned shot – 'I knew I had to hit a boundary, but there was little chance of getting one on the off-side, as Sussex had six fielders in a packed ring. With Arnold bowling the ball on middle-stump, I decided to swing across the line – if I had missed, it would have bowled me, but instead it went off the middle of the bat for six.' A match-winning stroke if ever there was one, and surely worthy of another flypast in celebration!

Eifion Jones

Peter Swart

Sussex won the toss and elected to bat *Umpires: F.R. Goodall and J.G. Langridge*

SUSSEX INNINGS

K.C. Wessels		b Lloyd	22
G.D. Mendis	c Richards	b Nash	26
Imran Khan	c Lloyd	b Swart	54
P.W.G. Parker	c and	b Swart	31
C.P. Phillipson	run out		14
S.J. Storey	c and	b Swart	11
A.C.S. Pigott		b Swart	2
*+ A. Long	not out		10
G.G. Arnold	not out		8
C.M. Wells			
R.G. Cheatle			
Extras		(LB 8, W 1, NB 1)	10
TOTAL		(for 7 wickets)	**188**

FOW: 1-44, 2-60, 3-134, 4-139, 5-164,
6-168, 7-177

Bowler	O	M	R	W
Nash	8	1	29	1
Wilkins	4	0	24	0
Lloyd	8	1	23	1
Richards	8	1	28	0
Swart	8	0	55	4
Ontong	4	0	19	0

GLAMORGAN INNINGS

*A. Jones		b Cheatle	39
J.A. Hopkins	c Cheatle	b Arnold	20
R.C. Ontong	c Storey	b Pigott	28
G. Richards	c Storey	b Pigott	9
P.D. Swart		b Storey	19
M.J. Llewellyn	c Mendis	b Imran	6
M.A. Nash	c Imran	b Arnold	27
+E.W. Jones	not out		19
D.A. Francis	run out		3
B.J. Lloyd	not out		7
A.H. Wilkins			
Extras		(B 2, LB 7, NB 3)	12
TOTAL		(for 8 wickets)	**189**

FOW: 1-33, 2-80, 3-96, 4-121, 5-122,
6-139, 7-171, 8-176

Bowling	O	M	R	W
Imran Khan	8	0	32	1
Arnold	7.5	0	51	2
Wells	5	1	26	0
Cheatle	8	2	17	1
Storey	7	0	32	1
Pigott	4	0	19	2

Glamorgan won by 2 wickets

ESSEX

There are some innings that simply defy description. The double-century by Javed Miandad against Essex at Colchester in 1981 is certainly in this category. His efforts came during a record-breaking season for the mercurial Pakistani batsman. During the summer, he amassed a club record 2,083 runs to finish the season with an average of 69.43 – the highest ever recorded by a Glamorgan batsman – whilst his tally of 8 centuries was also a new club record.

Javed's innings came during a game which Essex, pressing for the Championship, badly needed to win. But the home team began poorly as seamers Malcolm Nash and Simon Daniels took three wickets each, whilst Rodney Ontong took 4-37 with his fast-medium bowling. When Glamorgan batted, Javed Miandad and Norman Featherstone shared a partnership of 130 for the fourth wicket, before Miandad became one of six victims for Essex spinner David Acfield.

With a first innings lead of 87, and the wicketaking spin, Glamorgan appeared to be in the driving seat, but Essex openers Graham Gooch and Brian Hardie shared an opening stand of 169. Although Robin Hobbs took five wickets against his former employers, the other Glamorgan bowlers were simply overwhelmed by the Essex onslaught and failed to exploit the conditions.

The net result was that Glamorgan were left needing 325 in 323 minutes on the final day, and they were soon in deep trouble at 7-2, with Alan Jones and Rodney Ontong cheaply removed. But this only hastened the arrival of Javed Miandad, who came on to play what his colleagues and opponents alike later described as the finest innings they had ever seen.

Despite further losses, John Hopkins and Norman Featherstone, Javed farmed the strike and displayed a magical repertoire of shots, some bordering on the audacious, on a wicket that was giving the spinners lavish assistance. Time and again, Javed reverse-swept rising and turning balls, or flicked the bowler nonchalantly against the spin with a wicked grin on his face. After providing watchful support, Alan Lewis Jones and Eifion Jones fell to the spin combination of Acfield and East. Barry Lloyd soon followed, as well as Robin Hobbs – first ball, but not before Javed had taken

the score from 227 to 270, cheekily stealing a single at the end of every over, and protecting Hobbs for almost ten overs! Malcolm Nash and Simon Daniels also defended with spirit, forcing Keith Fletcher to recall his quicker bowlers in an attempt to halt Javed's dominance. Lever responded to his captain's call, dismissing both of the tailenders, leaving Miandad unbeaten on 200 and Glamorgan just 13 runs short of their target. The Pakistani genius left the field to a rousing ovation and handshakes from all of the Essex fielders, who had watched, almost in awe, Javed's single-handed mastery of their bowling. As one Essex stalwart said afterwards, 'the pitch was tinder dry and batting on it in the final innings was really impossible. Yet Javed never looked like getting out – it was as if he was batting on a different wicket. We simply could not believe our eyes.'

Javed Miandad in full flow!

Essex won the toss and elected to bat   *Umpires: D.G.L. Evans and K.E. Palmer*

ESSEX

1ST INNINGS				2ND INNINGS		
G.A. Gooch	lbw	b Nash	16	c A.L. Jones	b Lloyd	113
B.R. Hardie	c Daniels	b Ontong	37	not out		114
*K.W.R. Fletcher	lbw	b Daniels	6		b Ontong	6
K.S. McEwan	c E. Jones	b Daniels	0	c Miandad	b Ontong	2
A. Lilley	c Featherstone	b Ontong	14	c E.Jones	b Hobbs	88
N. Phillip	c Miandad	b Daniels	21	lbw	b Hobbs	4
S. Turner	lbw	b Nash	36	c Daniels	b Ontong	31
R.E. East .	c Daniels	b Ontong	19 (9)	c and	b Hobbs	4
+D.E. East	c Featherstone	b Nash	5 (8)	st E. Jones	b Hobbs	4
J.K. Lever	not out		14	st E. Jones	b Hobbs	9
D.L. Acfield	c Miandad	b Ontong	0			
Extras	(B 4, LB 6, W 6, NB 3)		19	(B 16, LB 15, W 4, NB 1)		36
TOTAL			**187**	(for 9 wkts dec)		**411**

FOW: 1-20, 2-29, 3-29, 4-69, 5-93,   1-169, 2-186, 3-188, 4-332, 5-341
          6-132, 7-152, 8-167, 9-174   6-388, 7-398, 8-402, 9-411

Bowling	O	M	R	W	Bowling	O	M	R	W
Nash	19	4	76	3	Nash	6	0	33	0
Daniels	11	3	33	3	Daniels	7	0	45	0
Ontong	13.4	2	37	4	Ontong	21	3	102	3
Lloyd	6	0	22	0	Lloyd	31	4	110	1
					Hobbs	21.5	3	85	5

GLAMORGAN

1ST INNINGS				2ND INNINGS		
A. Jones		b Lever	31	c D. East	b Lever	0
J.A. Hopkins	c Gooch	b Lever	46	c Fletcher	b Lever	16
R.C. Ontong	lbw	b Turner	5	c R. East	b Turner	4
Javed Miandad	st D. East	b Acfield	81	not out		200
N.G. Featherstone	st D. East	b R. East	59	c Fletcher	b Lever	0
A.L. Jones	c Gooch	b Acfield	15	lbw	b Acfield	36
+E.W. Jones	c Fletcher	b Acfield	1	st D. East	b R. East	24
*M.A. Nash	c Lever	b Acfield	10 (10)	c Turner	b Lever	1
B.J. Lloyd	lbw	b Acfield	4 (8)		b Acfield	0
S.A.B. Daniels	c Fletcher	b Acfield	2 (11)	lbw	b Lever	8
R.N.S. Hobbs	not out		6 (9)	c Fletcher	b Acfield	0
Extras	(B 2, LB 10, W 1, NB 1)		14	(B 12, LB 8, NB 2)		22
TOTAL			**274**			**311**

FOW: 1-56, 2-61, 3-99, 4-229, 5-229   1-0, 2-7, 3-44, 4-44, 5-155,
          6-232, 7-245, 8-262, 9-265   6-224, 7-227, 8-270, 9-291

Bowling	O	M	R	W	Bowling	O	M	R	W
Lever	19	3	59	2	Lever	17	2	62	5
Phillip	15	1	51	0	Philip	3	0	12	0
Turner	9	1	30	1	Turner	8	0	34	1
R. East	28	7	56	1	R. East	30	8	97	1
Acfield	24.5	8	64	6	Acfield	33	7	84	3

Essex won by 13 runs

NOTTINGHAMSHIRE

28, 29, 30 August 1985 at Trent Bridge

In 1983 Rodney Ontong, the South African-born all-rounder, changed bowling styles from pace to spin. He proved to be a prodigious spinner of the ball, claiming 74 wickets in 1984, during which he also took over the captaincy of a struggling Glamorgan side. The following year he produced a truly astonishing performance with an innings of 130 and 13 wickets in the match against Nottinghamshire to record one of the finest all-round efforts by a Glamorgan player.

Nottinghamshire had begun quite promisingly in their first innings and, entering the final half-hour on a rain-affected day, their score was 150-2, with captain Clive Rice leading the way with a brisk 63. But Rodney Ontong took four wickets in five dramatic overs, and all without conceding a run, as Nottinghamshire dramatically collapsed to 171-7.

They added only a further 27 runs on the second morning, before the Glamorgan batsmen produced an almost copybook performance of their opponents' first innings. After Alan Lewis Jones and John Hopkins gave the Welsh side a solid start, the home spinners, Eddie Hemmings and Peter Such, reduced Glamorgan to 81 for 4. But it was then Ontong the batsman who thwarted Nottinghamshire's progress, with 130 in 247 minutes. The Glamorgan captain was completely untroubled, hitting a six and 14 fours, as he counter-attacked in tandem with his uncapped partner, Matthew Maynard.

The young number six had scored a scintillating century on his county debut in the previous game at Swansea against Yorkshire, and the rookie batsman gave another uninhibited display of strokeplay, hitting ten crisp boundaries before he was yorked by seamer Andy Pick off the last ball of the afternoon's play. But it was only a temporary respite for the Nottinghamshire bowlers as Terry Davies and Mark Price gave Ontong further support as the Glamorgan captain reached a well-deserved century.

With a deficit of 131 in the first innings, the Nottinghamshire openers took the score to 59-0 before a dramatic collapse took place as Ontong claimed eight wickets whilst just another 61 runs were added. Wickets fell through tentative prods and indiscreet swipes against the turning balls from the Glamorgan captain. Ontong finished this classic contest with match figures of 13-106 and, quite fittingly, his name went into the notebooks of the England selectors. In 1987 he came very close to selection for England's World Cup party, but in August 1988 his fine career came to an abrupt end when he badly damaged his knee in a car crash en route to a game in Northamptonshire, and was forced into premature retirement.

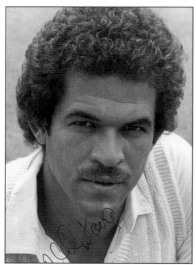

Rodney Ontong

Matthew Maynard celebrates his historic debut century against Yorkshire in 1985.

Nottinghamshire won the toss and elected to bat   Umpires: M.J. Kitchen and P.B. Wight

NOTTINGHAMSHIRE 1ST INNINGS

			2ND INNINGS			
B.C. Broad	c Jones	b Barwick	5		b Ontong	32
M. Newell	c Ontong	b Holmes	44		b Price	24
D.W. Randall		b Smith	32	c sub	b Ontong	0
*C.E.B. Rice	c Morris	b Ontong	63	c Jones	b Ontong	9
D. J. R. Martindale	lbw	b Ontong	4		b Ontong	1
J.D. Birch		b Barwick	22	lbw	b Ontong	3
+B.N. French	c Morris	b Ontong	0	c Hopkins	b Ontong	12
C.D. Fraser-Darling	c Holmes	b Ontong	0	(9) c Hopkins	b Price	8
R.A. Pick	c Davies	b Barwick	8	(10) not out		17
E.E. Hemmings	c Maynard	b Ontong	9	(8) c sub	b Ontong	4
P.M. Such	not out		0	c sub	b Ontong	0
Extras		(B 4, LB 5, NB 2)	11		(LB 5, W 5)	10
TOTAL			**198**			**120**

FOW: 1-10, 2-62, 3-150, 4-158, 5-159,
6-159, 7-163, 8-176, 9-195

1-59, 2-61, 3-63, 4-76, 5-77,
6-88, 7-97, 8-99, 9-118

Bowling	O	M	R	W	Bowling	O	M	R	W
Barwick	17.1	3	44	3	Barwick	6	2	11	0
Smith	12	3	39	1	Smith	4	0	10	0
Derrick	12	2	31	0	Ontong	18.3	3	67	8
Holmes	14	5	32	1	Price	20	6	27	2
Ontong	15	6	39	5					
Price	1	0	4	0					

GLAMORGAN INNINGS

A. Jones	c Birch	b Hemmings	35
J.A. Hopkins	c Newell	b Such	25
G.C. Holmes	c Fraser-Darling	b Hemmings	11
H. Morris	c Fraser-Darling	b Such	0
*R.C. Ontong	c Martindale	b Hemmings	130
M.P. Maynard		b Pick	58
+T. Davies	c Martindale	b Hemmings	21
M.R. Price	not out		28
J. Derrick	st French	b Hemmings	4
I. Smith		b Rice	4
S.R. Barwick	c French	b Pick	1
Extras		(LB 9, NB 3)	12
TOTAL			**329**

FOW: 1-59, 2-65, 3-65, 4-81, 5-203
6-260, 7-302, 8-309, 9-328

Bowling	O	M	R	W
Pick	17.2	5	54	2
Rice	15	3	28	1
Such	31	4	99	2
Hemmings	35	7	115	5
Fraser-Darling	4	0	24	0

Glamorgan won by an innings and 111 runs

WORCESTERSHIRE

21, 22, 23 July 1990 at Abergavenny

Many refer to 1990 as the 'Year of the Bat', as county bowlers laboured all summer with an experimental style of ball with a lower seam. The upshot was that batsmen the length and breadth of the country made hay as the sun shone, and some exceptionally high scoring contests were staged. This classic match between Glamorgan and Worcestershire at Abergavenny was no exception, as the Welsh county failed by just two runs to score a seemingly impossible target of 495, and on a placid pitch and sun-soaked outfield, the match saw 1,641 runs being made – a record aggregate for a three-day county match, and just 9 runs less than the Championship record, set in a four-day encounter at The Oval earlier in that summer.

The run-fest began with Worcestershire amassing 514-4 declared, with Graeme Hick, aged twenty-four, becoming the youngest batsman to score fifty first-class hundreds. Glamorgan then replied with 327-5, with captain Alan Butcher declaring as soon as Tony Cottey reached a well made hundred. When Worcestershire batted again, Hick added another century to his tally, taking his match aggregate to 592, and past Everton Weekes' previous record of 575 set in 1950.

Hick reached this landmark on the final morning as Phil Neale, the Worcestershire captain, batted on for a short while before setting Glamorgan a target of 495 in 88 overs. Despite the small boundaries on one of the country's most picturesque grounds, this was still a stiff target, especially given the fact that Glamorgan had rarely scored more than 300 to win a game.

Openers Alan Butcher and Hugh Morris were undaunted, adding 256 for the first wicket – their ninth century stand of a wonderful summer. Both made fine hundreds, but after this promising start four wickets quickly fell for 32, including Cottey and Maynard for just one apiece. However, Viv Richards was still at the crease and with a brisk 43 off just 18 balls, he reduced the requirement to 169 in the final 20 overs with 6 wickets in hand. With the scoring rate having risen to eight an over, Phil Neale knew that if Worcestershire were going to win, he needed to keep Glamorgan interested and to hopefully take wickets. Therefore, he brought on his occasional bowlers, and in six overs Nigel Cowley and Robert Croft smashed 75 runs. The regular bowlers came back on, but Cowley and Croft had extended their partnership to 124 in 15 overs when Cowley was caught behind off Ian Botham.

Robert Croft kept the attack going, even though 15 runs were still needed in the final over from Richard Illingworth. It looked as if Glamorgan might grab an amazing victory when Croft hit a huge six off the fourth ball. But the bowler, aiming wide of the leg stump, stifled Croft's ambition, and Glamorgan ended two runs short at the end of an amazing contest, which saw no less than 16 sixes and 249 fours being struck.

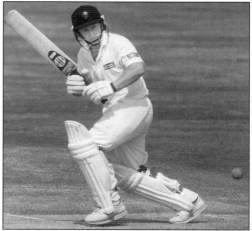

Left: Glamorgan's prolific openers, Hugh Morris and Alan Butcher, go out to bat from the Sophia Gardens dressing room. Right: Tony Cottey.

WORCESTERSHIRE 1ST INNINGS

T.S. Curtis		b Watkin	23		not out		111
P. Bent	c Cowley	b Croft	69	c Metson	b Watkin		79
G.A. Hick	not out		252		not out		100
D.B. D'Oliveira	c Maynard	b Cowley	121				
I.T. Botham	c Morris	b Bastien	29				
*P.A. Neale							
+S.J. Rhodes							
R.K. Illingworth							
P.J. Newport							
S.R. Lampitt							
N.V. Radford							

2ND INNINGS

	Extras	(B 9, LB 10, NB 1)	20		(LB 9, W 4, NB 4)	17
TOTAL		(for 4 wkts dec	**514**		(for 1 wkt dec)	**307**

FOW: 1-53, 2-157, 3-421, 4-514   1-132

Bowling	O	M	R	W	Bowling	O	M	R	W
Frost	18	0	109	0	Frost	11	0	38	0
Watkin	23	3	93	1	Watkin	19	1	109	1
Bastien	15.2	2	90	1	Bastien	12.3	2	61	0
Cowley	22	3	101	1	Cowley	1	0	1	0
Croft	12	0	71	1	Croft	10	0	61	0
Richards	7	0	31	0	Butcher	4	0	28	0

GLAMORGAN   1ST INNINGS

*A.R. Butcher		b Lampitt	79	c Neale	b Illingworth		130
H. Morris	lbw	b Botham	57	c Lampitt	b Newport		119
P.A. Cottey	not out		100 (5)	c D'Oliveira	b Newport		1
M.P. Maynard	c Lampitt	b Botham	15 (3)	c Hick	b Newport		1
I.V.A. Richards	c Rhodes	b Radford	41 (4)	c and	b Illingworth		43
R.D.B. Croft	c D'Oliveira	b Illingworth	28 (7)	not out			91
N.G. Cowley	not out		2 (6)	c Rhodes	b Botham		63
+C.P. Metson				not out			12
S.L. Watkin							
S. Bastien							
M. Frost							

2ND INNINGS

	Extras	(LB 1, NB 4)	5		(B 10, LB 21, NB 2)	33
TOTAL		(for 5 wkts dec)	**327**		(for 6 wkts)	**493**

FOW: 1-140, 2-144, 3-178, 4-248, 5-317   1-256, 2-257, 3-272, 4-288, 5-326, 6-450

Bowling	O	M	R	W	Bowling	O	M	R	W
Newport	15	0	72	0	Newport	19	4	87	3
Radford	15	1	79	1	Radford	12	1	67	0
Illingworth	15.1	2	80	1	Illingworth	24	2	124	2
Lampitt	11	2	40	1	Lampitt	3	1	14	0
Botham	12	1	55	2	Botham	12	2	40	1
Hick	1	1	0	0	Hick	12	3	61	0
Curtis	3	0	30	0					
D'Oliveira	3	0	39	0					

Match Drawn.

101

HAMPSHIRE

16, 18, 19 June 1990 at Southampton

This classic match, savaged by the loss of 86 overs on the second day, ended in the final over of the third day after Viv Richards had played a truly amazing innings, mixing controlled authority with some brutal strokeplay to steer Glamorgan to a memorable victory.

The easy-paced nature of the Southampton wicket was evident on the first day as Hampshire raced to 363-8, with Robin Smith hitting an impressive 153. However, persistent rain thwarted Glamorgan's reply on the second day, so after two declarations and successful negotiations between the captains, Mark Nicholas and Alan Butcher, Glamorgan were left with 102 overs on the final day to make 364. An asking rate of three and a half runs per over, and all day in which to chase the target, seemed a very generous one from the Hampshire captain. When Alan Butcher and Hugh Morris added 90 runs for the first wicket, Nicholas' boldness looked misplaced, but five wickets then fell in a disastrous spell after lunch as Glamorgan slumped to 139-5.

Viv Richards, the great West Indian batsman, was still unbeaten, however, and with ex-Hampshire spinner Nigel Cowley offering stubborn support, the pair took their partnership into the final hour, by which time the target had been reduced to 112 in 20 overs. With Malcolm Marshall running in at full throttle, Viv Richards needed to draw on all of his experience to keep Glamorgan in the hunt, and to protect his partner.

Cowley eventually fell for a brave 58, before wicketkeeper Colin Metson came in to lend Richards useful support. Even so, the target was still 12 runs from the final over of the match, and with Marshall the bowler, and Metson on strike, it looked as if Richards' brave innings would be in vain. Off the first delivery, Metson nurdled the ball to slip and scampered what seemed an impossible single. Richards then hit the next two balls for four and six – the latter shot a savage blow, which sent a good length ball from Marshall completely out of the ground.

But Richards was still not finished, as he stroked the next ball effortlessly to the boundary to see the Welsh county home with two balls to spare. He left the field unbeaten on 164 with 17 fours and 5 sixes, graciously acknowledging the applause from all of the players, and a standing ovation from the crowd, enraptured by the sheer brilliance and audacity of the West Indian batting maestro.

Viv Richards

Hampshire won the toss and elected to bat   *Umpires: J.W. Holder and B.J. Meyer*

HAMPSHIRE

		1ST INNINGS			2ND INNINGS	
V.P. Terry	c Metson	b Richards	52	not out		25
C.L. Smith	c Metson	b Watkin	48	not out		39
D.I. Gower	c Metson	b Watkin	41			
R.A. Smith	c Metson	b Frost	153			
M.D. Marshall	c Metson	b Dennis	4			
*M.C.J. Nicholas	c Cowley	b Watkin	30			
+R.J. Parks	c Metson	b Watkin	0			
R.J. Maru	c Maynard	b Cowley	9			
T.M. Tremlett	not out		14			
C.A. Connor						
P.J. Bakker						
Extras		(LB 10, W 1, NB 1)	12		(LB 5, W 1, NB 1)	7
TOTAL		(for 8 wkts dec)	**363**		(for 0 wkts dec)	**71**

FOW: 1-73, 2-127, 3-177, 4-182, 5-336
6-340, 7-341, 8-363

Bowling	O	M	R	W	Bowling	O	M	R	W
Frost	24	4	107	1	Smith	8	2	27	0
Watkin	30	9	84	4	Maynard	6	1	22	0
Dennis	20	5	83	1	Butcher	1.5	0	17	0
Cowley	17.5	6	47	1					
Richards	8	3	32	1					

GLAMORGAN

		1ST INNINGS			2ND INNINGS	
*A.R. Butcher	c Terry	b Bakker	7	c Connor	b Maru	51
H. Morris	not out		38	c Maru	b Connor	44
M.P. Maynard	not out		20	(4) c Gower	b Connor	1
G.C. Holmes				(3) c Terry	b Marshall	14
I.V.A. Richards				not out		164
I. Smith				c Parks	b Marshall	0
N.G. Cowley				c and	b Maru	58
+C.P. Metson				not out		14
S.J. Dennis						
S.L. Watkin						
M. Frost						
Extras		(B 1, LB 1, W 1, NB 3)	6		(B 5, LB 11, NB 5)	21
TOTAL		(for 1 wkt dec)	**71**		(for 6 wkts)	**367**

FOW: 1-31   1-90, 2-104, 3-106, 4-135, 5-139, 6-306

Bowling	O	M	R	W	Bowling	O	M	R	W
Marshall	3	1	9	0	Marshall	22.4	7	63	2
Bakker	4	0	14	1	Bakker	23	6	54	0
Tremlett	5	2	19	0	Tremlett	24	7	80	0
Nicholas	4.1	0	27	0	Connor	18	1	86	2
					Maru	14	2	68	2

Glamorgan won by 4 wickets

WARWICKSHIRE

20, 21, 22 May 1992 at Swansea

This early season game, played on a slow, turning Swansea wicket, saw Robert Croft display his match-winning qualities as an off-spinner. Many shrewd judges had forecasted a bright future for the twenty-one-year-old, who from a young age had been coached and advised by the wily Don Shepherd. The apprentice more than brought a smile to the face of the old sorcerer as he guided Glamorgan to their first win of the 1992 season, and one of the narrowest ever in the club's history.

The prelude to Croft's match-winning spell was an innings of 127 off 129 by Viv Richards, during century partnerships with Matthew Maynard and Tony Cottey. Glamorgan declared on 346-5, before Croft took six wickets in Warwickshire's first innings and, at one stage, it looked as if the visitors might even follow-on, but some determined batting by Andy Moles and some hefty blows by Neil Smith reduced Warwickshire's deficit to 98.

On the final day, Glamorgan extended their lead to 265 before declaring for a second time in the match. Left with 72 overs, Warwickshire were soon in trouble as opening bowlers Steve Watkin and Steve Bastien removed Jason Ratcliffe and Andy Lloyd. Things became even worse early in Robert Croft's spell as the young off-spinner bowled Neil Smith and Andy Moles to leave Warwickshire reeling on 34-4.

Roger Twose and Dermot Reeve then shared a gritty partnership, but one that was not without some luck at times, as Reeve unleased some unorthodox shots against the young bowler. Croft eventually reaped the reward for his steadiness, dismissing Twose and Michael Burns in quick succession. Paul Smith then lent Reeve some valuable support, and their stand of 69 in 30 overs seemed to have saved the game for the visitors.

Croft had the last laugh, however, having Reeve well caught by Steve Watkin with just seven overs to go. Paul Booth soon followed, and Warwickshire entered the final over of the game, to be bowled by Robert Croft, on 171-8. The off-spinner kept his nerve, having Paul Smith caught at short leg with his fourth delivery and then, with his next ball, Tim Munton was trapped leg before to give Croft career best figures of 14-169 and Glamorgan a quite enthralling victory.

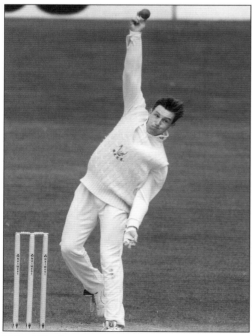

Robert Croft

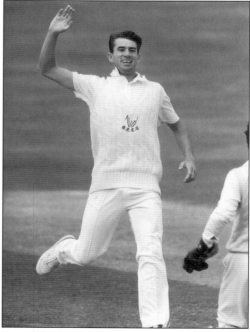

Steve Watkin

Glamorgan won the toss and elected to bat   *Umpires: G.I. Burgess and D.J. Constant*

GLAMORGAN   1ST INNINGS   2ND INNINGS

Batsman	Fielding 1st	Bowler 1st	R1		Fielding 2nd	Bowler 2nd	R2
S.P. James	c Burns	b Booth	26		c Munton	b N. Smith	35
H. Morris	lbw	b P. Smith	36		c Reeve	b Booth	28
A. Dale	c Reeve	b Twose	32		not out		67
*M.P. Maynard	c N.Smith	b Booth	62	(5) c Burns	b Donald	0
I.V.A. Richards	c Burns	b Twose	127				
P.A. Cottey		not out	42		c Burns	b Munton	9
R.D.B. Croft	not out		2		c Burns	b Munton	8
+C.P. Metson					not out		5
S.L. Watkin				(4) lbw		b Donald	1
S.R. Barwick							
S. Bastien							
Extras		(B 4, LB 8, NB 7)	19		(B 9, LB 3, NB 2)		14
TOTAL		(for 5 wkts dec)	346		(for 6 wkts dec)		167

FOW: 1-54, 2-80, 3-115, 4-226, 5-334   FOW: 1-68, 2-74, 3-92, 4-92, 5-126
6-146

Bowling	O	M	R	W	Bowling	O	M	R	W
Donald	12	3	51	0	Donald	14	4	24	2
Munton	24	8	44	0	Munton	14	3	43	2
Booth	32	4	129	2	Booth	8	3	27	1
P. Smith	19	5	52	1	N. Smith	26	5	61	1
Twose	6	0	22	2					
N. Smith	5	1	28	0					
Reeve	2	0	8	0					

WARWICKSHIRE   1ST INNINGS   2ND INNINGS

Batsman	Fielding 1st	Bowler 1st	R1		Fielding 2nd	Bowler 2nd	R2
A.J. Moles	c James	b Croft	66			b Croft	13
J.D. Ratcliffe	c Metson	b Watkin	9			b Watkin	1
*T.A. Lloyd	c James	b Croft	13			b Bastien	4
R.G. Twose	c and	b Croft	26	(6) c Maynard	b Croft	31
D.A. Reeve	c James	b Barwick	22	(4) c Watkin	b Croft	79
P.A. Smith	c Metson	b Barwick	25	(8) c James	b Croft	26
N.M.K. Smith		b Croft	67	(5)	b Croft	1
+M. Burns	c Richards	b Croft	3	(7) st Metson	b Croft	4
P.A. Booth	lbw	b Watkin	1		c Maynard	b Croft	0
A.A. Donald	not out		4		not out		1
T.A. Munton	c sub	b Croft	0		lbw	b Croft	0
Extras		(B 1, LB 8, NB 3)	12		(LB 11, NB 1)		12
TOTAL			248				172

FOW: 1-50, 2-74, 3-119, 4-134, 5-154,   1-5, 2-12, 3-30, 4-34, 5-88,
6-201, 7-216, 8-230, 9-248   6-92, 7-161, 8-169, 9-172

Bowling	O	M	R	W	Bowling	O	M	R	W
Bastien	15	5	44	0	Bastien	9	3	17	1
Watkin	16	5	38	2	Watkin	16	3	34	1
Croft	37.4	5	103	6	Croft	24.5	6	66	8
Barwick	18	5	54	2	Barwick	19	6	42	0
Cottey	3	2	2	0					

Glamorgan won by 93 runs

MIDDLESEX

1, 2, 3, 5 July 1993 at Cardiff

Few counties can ever have scored over 550 in their first innings and then lost the game, but this is precisely what happened to Glamorgan in this classic match, played at Cardiff in the first week of July 1993. At the time, Glamorgan and Middlesex were the top two sides in the Championship and the game looked like being a high scoring draw on a featherbed of a wicket.

Few could have predicted the drama ahead as Adrian Dale and Viv Richards shared a record-breaking partnership of 425 for the fourth wicket, as the Middlesex bowlers were firmly put to the sword, and all in glorious sunshine. Both Glamorgan batsmen hit unbeaten double-hundreds as they shared the highest ever stand for any wicket by the Welsh county, and at the time it was the seventh highest stand for the fourth wicket in the history of first-class cricket.

Yet despite the faultless strokeplay of Dale and Richards, and with Glamorgan passing the 550 mark, Middlesex still secured a first innings lead. Five of their batsmen passed fifty, including night-watchman John Emburey, who shared a stand of 262 with captain Mike Gatting. Even so, it was not until the final morning of the game that Middlesex gained the advantage and after an hour's batting they had secured a slender lead of 22.

When Glamorgan began their second innings at 12.10 p.m. on the final day, a draw looked almost certain. But England spinner Phil Tufnell then returned career-best bowling figures of 8-29, as Glamorgan dramatically collapsed. With clever flight and astute variations, the left-arm spinner took the first eight wickets to fall as just 60 runs were added, and Tufnell seemed poised to take all ten, before Cottey was run out and last man Steve Barwick fell to the off-spin of John Emburey.

This dramatic turnaround meant that Middlesex needed just 88 from 33 overs, and openers Desmond Haynes and Mike Roseberry had little difficulty in guiding their side to an emphatic ten-wicket victory: the Glamorgan spinners found nothing in the wicket on which Tufnell had woven an almost magical spell and created so much havoc in their own ranks.

Adrian Dale and Viv Richards leave the field at Sophia Gardens after their record-breaking stand.

GLAMORGAN   1ST INNINGS   2ND INNINGS

Batsman	1st dismissal	1st bowler	1st runs	2nd dismissal	2nd bowler	2nd runs
S.P. James	c Carr	b Tufnell	42		b Tufnell	11
*H. Morris	c Brown	b Williams	27	c Brown	b Tufnell	14
A. Dale	not out		214	lbw	b Tufnell	14
M.P. Maynard	c Gatting	b Feltham	14	c Carr	b Tufnell	32
I.V.A. Richards	not out		224	c Carr	b Tufnell	0
P.A. Cottey				run out		15
R.D.B. Croft				not out		2
+C.P. Metson				c Gatting	b Tufnell	0
R.P. Lefebvre					b Tufnell	0
S.L. Watkin				c Carr	b Tufnell	0
S.R. Barwick				c Carr	b Emburey	1
Extras	(B 4, LB 13, W 1, NB 23)		41	(B 6, LB 4, NB 10)		20
TOTAL	(for 3 wickets dec)		**562**			**109**

FOW: 1-50, 2-86, 3-137

1-25, 2-49, 3-62, 4-62, 5-95,
6-102, 7-102, 8-104, 9-104

Bowling	O	M	R	W	Bowling	O	M	R	W
Williams	26	5	85	1	Williams	3	0	16	0
Fraser	33	3	127	0	Fraser	3	2	2	0
Feltham	27	4	117	1	Emburey	23.2	6	52	1
Emburey	35	5	102	0	Tufnell	23	8	29	8
Tufnell	45	8	114	1					

MIDDLESEX   1ST INNINGS   2ND INNINGS

Batsman	1st dismissal	1st bowler	1st runs	2nd dismissal	2nd runs
D.L. Haynes	lbw	b Watkin	73	not out	50
M.A. Roseberry	c Cottey	b Watkin	58	not out	31
J.E. Emburey		b Dale	123		
*M.W. Gatting		b Lefebvre	173		
M.R. Ramprakash	c Morris	b Dale	4		
J.D. Carr	c Croft	b Watkin	18		
+K.R. Brown	not out		88		
M.A. Feltham	lbw	b Watkin	0		
N.F. Williams		b Croft	21		
A.R.C. Fraser	c Dale	b Croft	5		
P.C.R. Tufnell	c and	b Croft	5		
Extras	(B 9, LB 5, NB 2)		16	(B 4, LB 3)	7
TOTAL			**584**	(for 0 wickets)	**88**

FOW: 1-22, 2-135, 3-397, 4-441, 5-441,
6-493, 7-493, 8-561, 9-575

Bowling	O	M	R	W	Bowling	O	M	R	W
Watkin	31	4	87	4	Watkin	2	0	7	0
Lefebvre	30	8	72	1	Barwick	3	0	9	0
Barwick	44	14	131	0	Croft	8.4	2	45	0
Croft	54	9	174	3	Richards	6	0	20	0
Dale	22	6	55	2					
Richards	13	1	51	0					

Middlesex won by 10 wickets

WORCESTERSHIRE

22, 23, 24, 25 July 1993 at Worcester

Glamorgan's dramatic defeat by Middlesex at Sophia Gardens was one of the pivotal moments of the 1993 season. But the Glamorgan batsmen put this reverse behind them, and they continued to enjoy great success during the rest of the summer, ending the season in third place in the Championship, after winning 9 of their 17 games. It was their highest Championship position since 1970, and this summer, full of heady excitement, saw many exciting victories – none more so than in this classic contest against Worcestershire at New Road.

The match had a dramatic and nail-biting conclusion, and all after Colin Metson had established a new Glamorgan record with 8 dismissals. Darren Thomas, the eighteen-year-old pace bowler, was the pick of the Glamorgan attack in this, his first Championship appearance of the summer, with 9 wickets in the match.

Thomas' efforts put Glamorgan in a promising position after tea on the second day, but a defiant half-century by Phil Newport, plus a last wicket stand of 53 between Richard Illingworth and Neal Radford, swung the match back in Worcestershire's favour as the home side set Glamorgan a target of 331. Their position became stronger as Glamorgan slipped to 92-4 at lunch, and with promising opener Steve James missing the match through injury, it looked as if Glamorgan had little chance of winning.

But Adrian Dale, promoted to open after a fine summer at number three, had other ideas, and with support from David Hemp and Robert Croft, the game changed complexion once again in the afternoon session. The clatter of wickets at the start of the final hour seemed to have halted Glamorgan's chase, but Adrian Dale was undaunted and he continued to work the ball around, and reduced the deficit to 10 runs needed from five overs when he was dismissed by Stuart Lampitt.

Dale's efforts seemed to have won the game for Glamorgan, but with only one more run added, the ninth Welsh wicket fell, as Lampitt dismissed Steve Watkin, and a victory for Worcestershire now seemed a possibility. A draw or a tie were also possible and, with Richard Illingworth bowling the final over, it looked like a re-run of the 1990 match at Abergavenny. Darren Thomas, Glamorgan's novice number eleven, belied his inexperience and calmly strode to the wicket with the intention of hitting the winning runs. After some deft glides from Roland Lefebvre, Thomas duly swept Illingworth to the square-leg boundary to win the game with three deliveries still remaining.

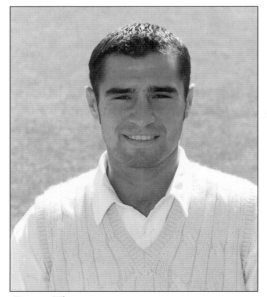

Darren Thomas

Adrian Dale

Worcestershire won the toss and elected to bat   Umpires: A.A. Jones and K.E. Palmer

WORCESTERSHIRE 1ST INNINGS

*T.S. Curtis	c Metson	b Thomas	45	lbw		b Watkin	45
W.P.C. Weston	c Metson	b Dale	39 (8)	c Metson		b Croft	1
G.A. Hick	c Dale	b Watkin	9	c Metson		b Watkin	9
D.B. D'Oliveira	c Hemp	b Thomas	73	c Cottey		b Thomas	13
M.J. Weston	c Richards	b Dale	4 (2)	c Richards		b Thomas	0
S.R. Lampitt	c Metson	b Thomas	18 (5)	c Metson		b Thomas	4
+S.J. Rhodes	c Metson	b Thomas	37 (6)	c and		b Dale	25
P.J. Newport		not out	20 (7)	c Richards		b Thomas	54
C.M. Tolley	c Metson	b Watkin	0	c Croft		b Watkin	7
R.K. Illingworth	c Metson	b Watkin	4	not out			42
N.V. Radford	c Morris	b Lefebvre	1			b Thomas	29
Extras		(LB 4, W 5, NB 8)	17		(B 1, LB 11, W 4, NB 2)		18
TOTAL			**267**				**247**

FOW: 1-84, 2-103, 3-105, 4-117, 5-152, 6-233, 7-250, 8-250, 9-260

1-12, 2-25, 3-49, 4-55, 5-78, 6-124, 7-141, 8-155, 9-194

Bowling	O	M	R	W	Bowling	O	M	R	W
Watkin	26	10	35	3	Watkin	26	7	63	3
Thomas	25	5	84	4	Thomas	23.3	2	76	5
Lefebvre	23.1	8	48	1	Lefebvre	22	9	30	0
Croft	18	6	47	0	Croft	21	8	39	1
Dale	19	7	49	2	Dale	9	1	27	1

GLAMORGAN 1ST INNINGS

A. Dale	c Curtis	b Tolley	44	c Radford	b Lampitt	124
*H. Morris	c Rhodes	b Newport	13	c M.J. Weston	b Tolley	15
M.P. Maynard	st Rhodes	b Illingworth	34	c Rhodes	b Newport	24
I.V.A. Richards	c Lampitt	b Newport	7	lbw	b Newport	0
P.A. Cottey	lbw	b Newport	4	c Curtis	b Lampitt	7
D.L. Hemp	c Hick	b Tolley	0		b Radford	52
R.D.B. Croft	c Hick	b Tolley	1	c Hick	b Illingworth	43
+C.P. Metson	c and	b Tolley	9	run out		22
R.P. Lefebvre	c Newport	b Illingworth	50	not out		18
S.L. Watkin	c D'Oliveira	b Illingworth	14	lbw	b Lampitt	0
S.D. Thomas	not out		5	not out		9
Extras	(LB 1, NB 2)		3	(LB 8, NB 12)		20
TOTAL			**184**	(for 9 wkts)		**334**

FOW: 1-23, 2-93, 3-100, 4-104, 5-104, 6-104, 7-106, 8-141, 9-175

1-28, 2-73, 3-79, 4-92, 5-180, 6-269, 7-293, 8-320, 9-321

Bowling	O	M	R	W	Bowling	O	M	R	W
Newport	19	5	55	3	Newport	21	4	60	2
Tolley	21	3	67	4	Tolley	10	3	42	1
Radford	7	0	35	0	Radford	8	2	26	1
Lampitt	5	0	15	0	Lampitt	26	5	84	3
Hick	3	1	9	0	Hick	6	1	19	0
Illingworth	6.4	4	2	3	Illingworth	26.3	3	81	1
M.J. Weston	5	0	14	0					

Glamorgan won by 1 wicket

KENT

The highlight of the 1993 season was Glamorgan's success in winning the AXA Equity and Law League – their first piece of silverware for almost a quarter of a century. For several years, the Welsh county had hinted at being a useful one-day unit. The acquisition of Roland Lefebvre from Somerset gave their attack an extra dimension, and his signing yielded immediate dividends as Lefebvre delivered some miserly spells with the new ball.

Another factor was that the other young players had reached maturity and, under Hugh Morris' enterprising captaincy, the Glamorgan side acquired the habit of winning one-day games early in June. By the end of August, they had became accustomed to the taste of success, putting together twelve consecutive victories, and made a mockery of their pre-season odds of 500-1.

Glamorgan's success was also based on consistent batting, with Hugh Morris leading by example with 737 runs during the season, and the astute captain formed a fine opening pair with Steve James. Their successful partnership was in stark contrast to other counties, who promoted tailenders as pinch-hitters to take advantage of the new rules for just two outfielders in the opening fifteen overs. But Morris and James showed the virtue of having two specialist batsmen to exploit the gaps in the field. With Matthew Maynard at number three, Viv Richards at number four, Adrian Dale at number five, and Tony Cottey coming in at six, Glamorgan had a highly effective top order.

On the bowling front, Steve Watkin and Roland Lefebvre proved to be amongst the most economical of new ball attacks. They were then supported by the clever off-cutters of Steve Barwick and the subtle off-breaks of Robert Croft, who tricked and teased the opponents and, more often than not, harried them into taking risks and perishing to a rash stroke.

As in 1948 and 1969, Glamorgan's bowlers were supported by some fine performances in the

Tony Cottey and Viv Richards sprint off the pitch at Canterbury after Glamorgan had become Sunday League champions.

Roland Lefebvre takes a vital catch – the Dutchman's superb fielding and accurate bowling were a vital ingredient in Glamorgan's success in 1993.

field, and they owed a huge debt of gratitude to their enthusiastic fielders, many of whom pulled off some stunning catches. At forty-one, Viv Richards was often the oldest player in the match, yet he rarely looked it, with some superb ground fielding, athletic catches and the running out of several opponents who foolishly thought they could steal a run to the old warhorse!

Glamorgan had never before finished above fifth place in the Sunday League; during the previous three seasons they had been rooted near the base of the table, winning 14 games and losing 43. This dismal record was dispelled by a truly collective effort in 1993, and their fine batting, superb bowling and outstanding fielding saw Glamorgan rise to the unfamiliar, heady heights of being Sunday League leaders in early July.

For the next ten weeks they remained at the top of the table, and stayed in a dog-fight with Kent by virtue of winning every game from 6 June until 12 September. Their winning sequence ended amongst heavy rain at Cardiff after Essex had been reduced to 7-2. This washout left Glamorgan level on points with Kent, but behind them on run-rate. By a quirk of fate, the two counties met at Canterbury on the final Sunday of the season, in a head-to-head showdown for the title.

From an early hour, the St Lawrence ground was buzzing with Welsh voices, eager to see Glamorgan, at long last, bring an end to their dismal record in one-day cricket, and also to cheer on Viv Richards as the great West Indian cricketer brought the curtain down on his glittering career. They were not disappointed on either count, as Glamorgan recorded a famous victory that even the most skilful of scriptwriters would have been hard pressed to devise for poignancy.

Kent won the toss and on a slow, low pitch had reached a quite promising 168-4 with ten overs left. It seemed as if the Welshmen would be chasing a target well over 200 until Steve Watkin and Roland Lefebvre induced a late order collapse which saw Kent falter and lose 5 wickets for 14 runs, leaving Glamorgan a target of 201. Alan Igglesden raised Kent's spirits by removing Steve James with just 6 runs on the board, but Hugh Morris and Adrian Dale skilfully saw off the new ball attack, adding 78 for the second wicket, before both fell attempting to force the pace. When Matthew Maynard was trapped lbw, Kent seemed to be in the ascendancy with Glamorgan on

141-4. But Viv Richards had come in to a spontaneous standing ovation from the crowd of 12,000 and, with Tony Cottey quietly playing himself in, the pair kept Glamorgan's hopes alive.

Even so, there were still a few heart-stopping moments, the first one coming when Richards was hit on the chest by Duncan Spencer, Kent's Anglo-Australian pace bowler. When the West Indian was caught off a bouncer, it looked as if Spencer had dealt a match-winning blow for his adopted county – but the umpire called no-ball (to a roar of delight from the Welsh supporters) and Richards remained at the crease.

This was the defining moment of an enthralling match, as from this point on, everything went in Glamorgan's favour: the Cottey-Richards partnership grew, and Kentish spirits started to wilt. The pair added 60 in ten overs before Cottey top-edged Spencer high over the head of wicketkeeper Steve Marsh, and as the ball sped to the unguarded boundary, the two Glamorgan batsmen ran off, punching the air with sheer delight. It was not long before both the champagne and the tears were flowing in the Glamorgan dressing room, and the city of Canterbury witnessed a memorable night of jubilant celebrations by the Welsh team and their joyous supporters.

Above left: Steve Barwick.
Above right: Hugh Morris.
Left: Hugh Morris and
Matthew Maynard
embrace each other in the
Canterbury dressing room.

KENT INNINGS

T.R. Ward	c Metson	b Watkin	11
M.V. Fleming	c Morris	b Croft	44
C.L. Hooper	c Dale	b Barwick	60
N.J. Llong		b Dale	25
M.A. Ealham	lbw	b Croft	13
G.R. Cowdrey	c Metson	b Dale	10
*+S.A. Marsh	c Lefebvre	b Watkin	6
D.J. Spencer	c Richards	b Watkin	5
D.P. Fulton	c and	b Lefebvre	1
D.W. Headley	not out		10
A.P. Igglesden	not out		6
Extras		(LB 8, NB 1)	9
TOTAL		(for 9 wkts)	**200**

FOW:　　1-29, 2-72, 3-103, 4-123, 5-168, 6-170, 7-180, 8-180, 9-182

Bowling	O	M	R	W
Lefebvre	10	0	43	1
Watkin	10	1	33	3
Barwick	10	1	33	1
Croft	10	1	42	2
Dale	10	1	41	2

GLAMORGAN INNINGS

S.P. James	c Cowdrey	b Igglesden	3
*H. Morris	c Fleming	b Ealham	67
A. Dale	c Marsh	b Headley	31
M.P. Maynard	lbw	b Spencer	2
I.V.A. Richards	not out		46
P.A. Cottey	not out		33
Extras		(B 7, LB 1, W 7, NB 4)	19
TOTAL		(for 4 wkts)	**201**

DNB:　　R.D.B. Croft, +C.P. Metson, R.P. Lefebvre, S.L. Watkin, S.R. Barwick

FOW:　　1-6, 2-84, 3-98, 4-141

Bowling	O	M	R	W
Igglesden	10	1	43	1
Ealham	10	3	20	1
Headley	10	0	43	1
Hooper	9	0	44	0
Spencer	8.4	1	43	1

Glamorgan won by 2 wickets

HAMPSHIRE

9 July 1997 at Southampton

There were a host of exciting contests in 1997, both in one-day games and the Championship fixtures, as the Welsh county enjoyed perhaps their most successful ever all-round season. On the one-day front, Glamorgan progressed to the semi-final of the NatWest Trophy, although earlier in the summer it had looked as if Glamorgan would make a hasty exit from the competition when they were set a challenging target of 303 to beat Hampshire at Southampton.

This proved to be a truly classic one-day encounter, with the initiative swinging one way and then the other, before the game was decided in the final over. The match began with Hampshire being put in on a excellent wicket at the Northlands Road ground. Robin Smith struck an elegant hundred to set the Welsh side a quite daunting target, with the asking rate at a fraction over five an over.

When tea was taken after 25 overs, Glamorgan had made a solid start with their score on 113-1, but the loss of three quick wickets within the space of six overs saw their fortunes take a turn for the worse. When the fifth wicket fell with the score on 192, Hampshire seemed well on top, with 111 runs still being needed and just sixteen overs left.

But Glamorgan had successfully modified their batting order, with Steve James batting at number six to capitalise on his strength of deft placement and swift running between the wickets. James was joined at the crease by wicketkeeper Adrian Shaw, and with a combination of clever nudges and forcing strokes, they reduced the target to 62 in eight overs.

Then followed a moment of controversy, as Shaun Udal appeared to gather a throw from Matthew Hayden to run out Shaw. The wicketkeeper trudged off dejectedly, but after several moments of confusion, he was recalled by umpire Ray Julian, after Udal had admitted that he had not got the ball in his grasp when breaking the wicket.

It was at this point that the match seemed to finally turn in Glamorgan's favour, although there were still a few nerve-racking moments before a famous victory was won. Shaw and James added a further 51 in just six overs, before James was dismissed with twelve runs still needed. Darren Thomas was then quickly dismissed, but Waqar Younis, Glamorgan's overseas player, drew on his experience of playing in tense one-day internationals. Amidst mounting excitement, the Pakistani pace bowler and the defiant Adrian Shaw calmly knocked off the winning runs, to see the Welsh county home with just two balls to spare.

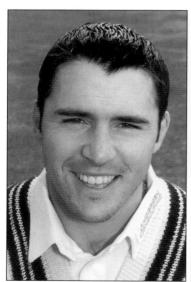

Adrian Shaw

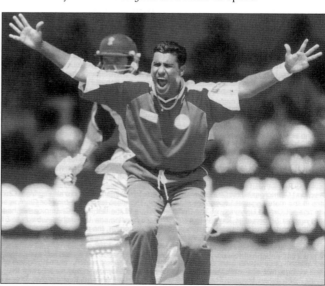

How could an umpire say no – Waqar Younis appeals!

Glamorgan won the toss and elected to bowl   *Umpires: R. Julian and B.J. Meyer*

HAMPSHIRE INNINGS

J.S. Laney	c James	b Dale	35
M.L. Hayden	lbw	b Thomas	20
R.A. Smith	c Maynard	b Thomas	119
M. Keech	c Morris	b WaqarYounis	34
W.S. Kendall	c Cottey	b Watkin	16
*J.P. Stephenson	lbw	b Croft	1
S.D. Udal	not out		39
+A.N. Aymes	not out		11
Extras		(B 3, LB 10, W 14)	27
TOTAL		(for 6 wkts)	**302**

DNB: R.J. Maru, S.J. Renshaw, C.A. Connor
FOW: 1-45, 2-101, 3-149, 4-193, 5-194, 6-277

Bowling	O	M	R	W
Waqar Younis	12	0	62	1
Watkin	12	1	44	1
Thomas	11	0	70	2
Croft	12	1	30	1
Dale	9	0	61	1
Cottey	4	0	22	0

GLAMORGAN INNINGS

R.D.B. Croft	c Laney	b Renshaw	0
H. Morris	run out		53
A. Dale	c Aymes	b Connor	71
*M.P. Maynard	c Keech	b Stephenson	30
P.A. Cottey	c Hayden	b Stephenson	5
S.P. James	c Aymes	b Connor	69
G.P. Butcher	c Aymes	b Stephenson	11
+A.D. Shaw	not out		34
S.D. Thomas	c Udal	b Renshaw	1
Waqar Younis	not out		8
Extras		(LB 12, W 10)	22
TOTAL		(for 8 wkts)	**304**

DNB: S.L. Watkin
FOW:1-0, 2-128, 3-132, 4-144, 5-192, 6-215, 7-291, 8-292

Bowling	O	M	R	W
Renshaw	12	1	71	2
Connor	11.4	1	55	2
Maru	11	0	55	0
Stephenson	12	1	49	3
Udal	12	0	56	0
Keech	1	0	6	0

Glamorgan won by 2 wickets

The NatWest Trophy quarter-final between Glamorgan and Yorkshire at Cardiff saw the Welsh side win another tense game by the narrow margin of one wicket, and all despite losing seven wickets in mid-innings for just 69 runs. A last wicket partnership of 28 between Waqar Younis and Dean Cosker saw Glamorgan through to a semi-final encounter – against Essex at Chelmsford. After the nail-biting victories at Southampton and at Sophia Gardens, surely the game against Essex would not be as dramatic? In fact the match was, if anything, even more thrilling as it spilled over into the reserve day after a cliff-hanger of an end to the first day.

Morning rain saw the loss of an hour's play but, despite this interruption, opener Steve James anchored the Glamorgan innings with a fine 109, and shared a century partnership with his close friend Adrian Dale. Tony Cottey also made a gutsy half-century, as Glamorgan's innings finished on 301-8. If Essex were going to win, they needed a good start, and this is precisely what they got – Australian Stuart Law and Darren Robinson shared a century opening stand in the first 15 overs and by the tea-break Essex appeared well placed at 157-1.

After the interval, Steve Watkin made two important breakthroughs, dismissing Robinson and Nasser Hussain, before Ronnie Irani and Paul Grayson added 61 for the fourth wicket to put Essex back into a favourable position. Matthew Maynard then made another important bowling change, bringing on Darren Thomas, and the young pace bowler took 4 for 14 in 19 balls to set up an intriguing finale.

By this time the light was starting to fade and the tension was mounting – so much so that there was a confrontation, caught by the television cameras (and subsequently over-publicised), between Mark Illot and Robert Croft. With nerves on a knife-edge and Waqar Younis back into the attack, the umpires took the players off the field at 8.10 p.m. with the home side requiring a further six runs from the remaining 41 balls, and Glamorgan two more wickets to win a pulsating contest.

Play resumed the following day, with Waqar Younis completing his over before Darren Thomas had Tim Hodgson caught behind with his first ball of the day. Essex were 299-9, and striding to the wicket was their number eleven, Peter Such, who had few pretensions as a batsman. Somehow he survived the next four deliveries, before hitting the final ball of the over to the boundary to see Essex home and to a place in the final against Warwickshire.

Steve James

Darren Thomas in his delivery stride.

Essex won the toss and elected to field   Umpires: J.C. Balderstone and D.J. Constant

GLAMORGAN INNINGS

S.P. James	c Robinson	b Grayson	109
H. Morris	c S. Law	b Cowan	6
A. Dale	c Cowan	b Grayson	45
*M.P. Maynard	run out		26
P.A. Cottey	c Grayson	b Ilott	56
R.D.B. Croft	run out		14
G.P. Butcher	not out		18
+A.D. Shaw	run out		1
S.D. Thomas	c S. Law	b Cowan	1
Waqar Younis			
S.L. Watkin			
Extras		(LB 9, W 10, NB 6)	25
TOTAL		(for 8 wkts)	**301**

FOW: 1-13, 2-115, 3-165, 4-251, 5-276, 6-291, 7-294, 8-301

Bowling	O	M	R	W
Ilott	12	2	50	1
Cowan	12	0	62	2
Irani	9.2	0	36	0
S.Law	5.4	0	37	0
Such	12	0	56	0
Grayson	9	0	51	2

ESSEX INNINGS

D.D.J. Robinson	c Cottey	b Watkin	62
S.G. Law .	c Waqar Younis	b Butcher	90
*N. Hussain	c Maynard	b Watkin	28
R.C. Irani	lbw	b Thomas	51
A.P. Grayson	c Shaw	b Thomas	22
D.R. Law		b Thomas	17
+R.J. Rollins	c James	b Thomas	2
A.P. Cowan	run out		2
T.P. Hodgson	c Shaw	b Thomas	2
M.C. Ilott	not out		1
P.M. Such	not out		4
Extras		(B 4, LB 6, W 6, NB 6)	22
TOTAL		(for 9 wkts)	**303**

FOW:1-150, 2-194, 3-195, 4-256, 5-280, 6-286, 7-295, 8-295, 9-299

Bowling	O	M	R	W
Watkin	12	1	64	2
Waqar Younis	9	1	48	0
Thomas	12	0	74	5
Croft	12	0	47	0
Butcher	7	0	39	1
Dale	3	0	21	0

Essex won by 1 wicket

SOMERSET

18, 19, 20 September 1997 at Taunton

Glamorgan become County Champions for the third time in their history in 1997. Throughout the season, Matthew Maynard's team displayed tenacity and positive endeavour, and their collective efforts were shrewdly marshalled by new coach Duncan Fletcher, the former Zimbabwe all-rounder. His wise advice and shrewd analysis helped many of the younger players to improve their game, whilst Maynard's imaginative leadership saw Glamorgan win eight of their seventeen Championship fixtures.

Waqar Younis was the club's overseas player and he proved to be a talisman in Glamorgan's success. The Pakistani pace ace handsomely repaid the money invested in him, taking 68 wickets at just 22 apiece. During June, he also produced two match-winning performances, with 8-17 against Sussex at Swansea and a hat-trick against Lancashire at Liverpool in a stunning victory which put the Welsh county at the top of the table.

The presence of Waqar also meant that long-serving seamer Steve Watkin no longer had to shoulder the burden of being both strike and stock bowler. Watkin had another fine season, and with Darren Thomas improving in leaps and bounds under Duncan Fletcher's tutelage, Glamorgan had an impressive pace attack. In the spin department, Robert Croft was partnered

Three of the key figures in the Championship success – captain Matthew Maynard, coach Duncan Fletcher and overseas bowler Waqar Younis.

Matthew Maynard and the delighted Glamorgan team celebrate the Championship win on the balcony at Taunton.

by the promising left-arm spin of Dean Cosker and, overall, the county possessed an attack that could prosper on every type of surface.

On the batting front, Steve James had an *annus mirabilis*, amassing 1,775 first-class runs, to become the country's leading run scorer of the season. He also formed a wonderful opening partnership with the ever-dependable Hugh Morris, who began the season with a career-best 233 against Warwickshire, and ended it against Somerset with his 52nd century for the county to draw level with Alan Jones' club record. His record-equalling feat came at Taunton as the Welsh county travelled to the West Country, leading the Championship by one point from Kent and needing fair weather and the small matter of a maximum 24 points to make sure of their first Championship title since 1969.

After winning the toss, Matthew Maynard invited Somerset to bat first and, despite suffering from a throat infection, Waqar claimed four wickets to dismiss the home side for 252. Andy Caddick took two early wickets, but Morris and Maynard saw off the new ball and proceeded to share a superb partnership of 235 for the third wicket.

Their stand was achieved at a helter-skelter pace of six runs an over and, even more remarkably, the pair of Glamorgan batsmen kept up their brisk scoring rate in appalling light on the second day and after a break for rain – at times all five lights were brightly shining on the scoreboard meter. Maynard gave an exhilarating display of controlled hitting, with the Glamorgan captain racing to a glorious century without even making a single. When he finally fell for 142, his breath-taking innings had lasted just 117 balls, and had contained 28 fours and a six.

Hugh Morris continued resolutely at the other end, and consolidated the good work on the next morning, as Glamorgan advanced from their overnight 353-4 to a formidable 527. Morris was eventually dismissed for 165, with 28 crisply struck boundaries, before Robert Croft and Adrian Shaw each chipped in with robust half-centuries to give Glamorgan full bonus points and a healthy first innings lead of 275.

Somerset began their second innings after lunch, but their batsmen then feasted on some wayward new ball bowling. A fine spell from Darren Thomas changed things, as the young bowler took five wickets and consistently beat the Somerset batsmen with his pace and control. At 166-7, the Welsh spectators started to celebrate, but their actions proved rather premature as Graham Rose and Andy Caddick shared a defiant stand of 95 in 14 overs. The ever reliable Steve Watkin returned to end the Somerset fightback, having Rose caught behind before adding the scalp of number eleven Kevin Shine.

Dean Cosker then trapped Ben Trott leg before to leave Glamorgan needing just 11 to win. It took only eight deliveries before Steve James hit the winning boundary and, despite Kent defeating Surrey, Glamorgan had secured a full compliment of bonus points, their ten-wicket victory giving Matthew Maynard's men a well-deserved Championship title and Glamorgan's first for twenty-eight years.

The team of 1997 celebrate on the outfield at Taunton after beating Somerset to win the County Championship – a great day for Glamorgan and Wales!

Glamorgan won the toss and elected to bowl   *Umpires: G. Sharp and P. Willey*

SOMERSET

	1ST INNINGS				2ND INNINGS		
+R.J. Turner	c Thomas	b Watkin	40		b Thomas	38	
P.C.L. Holloway		b Waqar	0	c Shaw	b Thomas	25	
S.C. Ecclestone	c Morris	b Waqar	0	c Morris	b Watkin	10	
M.N. Lathwell		b Waqar	62		b Thomas	47	
M.E. Trescothick	c Maynard	b Croft	20	c James	b Croft	16	
M. Burns		b Waqar	28	c Shaw	b Thomas	18	
*P.D. Bowler	c Morris	b Watkin	63	lbw	b Thomas	3	
G.D. Rose	lbw	b Cosker	13	c Shaw	b Watkin	67	
A.R. Caddick	c Croft	b Cosker	11	not out		56	
K.J. Shine	c Morris	b Watkin	6	c James	b Watkin	0	
B.J. Trott	not out		1	lbw	b Cosker	0	
Extras		(LB 6, NB 2)	8		(LB 3, NB 2)	5	
TOTAL			**252**			**285**	

FOW: 1-17, 2-17, 3-72, 4-113, 5-155, 6-156, 7-197, 8-217, 9-251

FOW: 1-60, 2-67, 3-88, 4-133, 5-145, 6-153, 7-166, 8-261, 9-273

Bowling	O	M	R	W	Bowling	O	M	R	W
Waqar	12	3	41	4	Waqar	11	0	84	0
Watkin	13.4	2	61	3	Watkin	15	1	75	3
Thomas	16	2	53	0	Thomas	15	2	38	5
Cosker	14	3	42	2	Cosker	11.4	3	34	1
Croft	13	1	49	1	Croft	18	5	51	1

GLAMORGAN

	1ST INNINGS				2ND INNINGS	
S.P. James	lbw	b Caddick	8	not out		9
H. Morris		b Caddick	165	not out		1
A. Dale	c Bowler	b Caddick	8			
*M.P. Maynard	c Bowler	b Shine	142			
P.A. Cottey	c Bowler	b Shine	13			
R.D.B. Croft	lbw	b Rose	86			
+A.D. Shaw	not out		53			
S.D. Thomas	c Ecclestone	b Trott	0			
Waqar Younis	c Ecclestone	b Trott	5			
S.L. Watkin	c Shine	b Trott	5			
D.A. Cosker		b Caddick	7			
Extras		(LB 7, W 12, NB 16)	35		(LB 1)	1
TOTAL			**527**		(for 0 wkts)	**11**

FOW: 1-12, 2-42, 3-277, 4-293, 5-404, 6-475, 7-476, 8-482, 9-495

Bowling	O	M	R	W	Bowling	O	M	R	W
Caddick	34.4	5	132	4	Caddick	1	0	5	0
Shine	17	3	88	2	Rose	0.2	0	5	0
Rose	29	3	152	1					
Trott	11	0	74	3					
Burns	7	0	65	0					
Bowler	1	0	9	0					

Glamorgan won by 10 wickets

SURREY

27, 28 May 2000 at Cardiff

The 2000 season saw Glamorgan reach their second Lord's final, and this followed a fine run by the Welsh county in the Benson & Hedges competition, staged during a soggy May and June. Despite defeat in the zonal game at Worcester, Glamorgan progressed to the quarter-final stages where they demolished Hampshire at Cardiff, beating the visitors by 113 runs after the English county had been dramatically bowled out for just 69. This victory saw Glamorgan secure a home tie in the semi-final against Surrey, held once again at their impressively redeveloped headquarters at Sophia Gardens. However, rain interfered with the contest, after Matthew Maynard had opted to bat first on a slow Cardiff wicket. Only 24.1 overs were possible on the first day, before Matthew Maynard and Mike Powell consolidated Glamorgan's position with a stand of 133 in 27 overs.

Maynard's batting was the epitome of a positive approach and, early in his innings, he advanced down the pitch to straight drive the wayward Ben Hollioake for an effortless six. Powell added three boundaries in another loose over from the Surrey bowlers and, despite the damp outfield, their stand galvanised Glamorgan's efforts. Maynard had played a perfect captain's innings, hitting a century off 109 balls and, despite a tail-end collapse, Glamorgan were able to set the visitors a challenging target of 252.

The Londoners were soon in trouble as Owen Parkin, in a controlled new ball spell, dismissed the dangerous Ally Brown and then pinch-hitter Alex Tudor. Mark Butcher and Alec Stewart subsequently steadied proceedings, before Robert Croft and Alex Wharf made decisive breakthroughs. These came just as the rain clouds were gathering over the Cardiff ground, and the Surrey batsmen, aware of their side's poor position under the Duckworth-Lewis system, appeared to be unsure whether to improve their run-rate by going for quick runs or to keep pushing the singles in the hope that the game would go the full distance.

After a brief stoppage for rain, they opted for quick runs and a flurry of wickets followed as Glamorgan remained on top. Despite some brave blows from Jason Ratcliffe and Martin Bicknell, Glamorgan had enough runs in the bank, and when Alec Stewart cut the ball to Steve James at point, their innings ended 33 runs short of the target.

Left: Alex Wharf appeals successfully against Surrey captain Adam Hollioake. Right: Owen Parkin.

Glamorgan won the toss and elected to bat   Umpires: D.J. Constant and J.W. Holder
TV umpire: V.A. Holder

GLAMORGAN INNINGS

R.D.B. Croft	c and	b Tudor	1
M.T.G. Elliott		b Bicknell	6
M.J. Powell		b Tudor	67
*M.P. Maynard	c Salisbury	b A.J. Hollioake	109
A. Dale	run out		25
S.P. James	not out		10
K. Newell		b A.J. Hollioake	6
A.G. Wharf	run out		0
+A.D. Shaw		b A.J. Hollioake	0
S.L. Watkin	run out		1
O.T. Parkin	run out		0
Extras		(LB 14, W 10, NB 2)	26
Total			**251**

FOW: 1-3, 2-27, 3-160, 4-226, 5-231,
6-241, 7-250, 8-250, 9-251

Bowling	O	M	R	W
Bicknell	10	0	40	1
Tudor	10	2	46	2
B.C. Hollioake	7.1	0	49	0
Ratcliffe	7	0	26	0
Salisbury	8	0	40	0
A.J. Hollioake	7	0	36	3

SURREY INNINGS

M.A. Butcher	st Shaw	b Croft	32
A.D. Brown	c Elliott	b Parkin	0
A.J. Tudor	lbw	b Parkin	0
+A.J. Stewart	c James	b Parkin	85
G.P. Thorpe		b Wharf	21
*A.J. Hollioake	lbw	b Wharf	1
B.C. Hollioake	c Newell	b Wharf	4
I.J. Ward		b Croft	2
J.D. Ratcliffe	c Dale	b Croft	24
M.P. Bicknell	c James	b Parkin	25
I.D.K. Salisbury	not out		0
Extras		(LB 13, W 5)	18
Total			**212**

FOW: 1-11, 2-11, 3-65, 4-101, 5-105,
6-121, 7-125, 8-170, 9-201

Bowling	O	M	R	W
Parkin	8	0	60	4
Watkin	9	0	30	0
Wharf	9	0	37	3
Dale	7	0	30	0
Croft	10	0	42	3

Glamorgan won by 32 runs (D/L method)

GLOUCESTERSHIRE

10 June 2000 at Lord's

Glamorgan's victory over Surrey gave the Welsh side their first Lord's final for twenty-three years, so 12 June 2000 was 'Daffodil Day' as their supporters, from far and wide, descended on the famous ground hoping to see Matthew Maynard's side lift the Benson & Hedges Cup. According to their patriotic script, this was to be the day when the inspirational Glamorgan leader would take a piece of silverware back to Wales, from the very heart of English cricket.

Sadly, it was not to be, but this classic match saw Maynard become the first ever batsman in cricket history to score a century in both the semi-final and final of a major one-day competition. He arrived at the crease with the scoreboard showing 24-2, after Australian all-rounder Ian Harvey had dismissed fellow Aussie, Matthew Elliott, and pinch-hitter Robert Croft. Once again, the Glamorgan captain found himself at the crease in a major game with Mike Powell, and the pair repeated their efforts in the semi-final by adding 137 in 31 overs.

As before, Maynard gave a disciplined and cultured display of strokeplay that was ultimately to give the Glamorgan captain the solace of the Gold Award. His well-timed strokes and deft placement transformed the scoreboard to 161-2, when Powell was caught and bowled by Jeremy Snape. There were still plenty of overs in hand for the other Glamorgan batsmen to give Maynard further support, but the innings fell away, as Harvey returned to strangle the lower order.

With the score on 225, Matthew Maynard was run out in the final over after a direct hit by Kim Barnett and, as the Glamorgan batsmen walked off to a standing ovation and handshakes from all of the Gloucestershire fielders, Glamorgan's supporters knew in their heart of hearts the Welsh side were twenty or thirty runs short of a good score.

Maynard then led his side back onto the Lord's ground, knowing that if Glamorgan were going to win the Benson & Hedges Cup, he needed to take early wickets. This was not to be: Tim Hancock and the vastly experienced Kim Barnett feasted on the Glamorgan new ball bowling, and by the time Robert Croft came on in the 14th over, 72 runs were already on the board. The scoring rate slowed and, in trying to force the pace, Barnett played on to a delivery by Croft. Steve Watkin returned to take the wicket of Rob Cunliffe and, when Owen Parkin clung on to a fierce return catch, Gloucestershire had slipped to 131-3 after 30 overs.

Any slim hopes of a Welsh victory were finally extinguished by a brisk partnership of 95 in 17 overs by Matt Windows and captain Mark Alleyne. It steered Gloucestershire to victory by seven wickets and their win, achieved with 19 balls in hand, was their third successive victory in a one-day final – a feat unmatched by any other county.

Matthew Maynard kisses his helmet and then acknowledges the applause after his century in the final.

Glamorgan won the toss and elected to bat

GLAMORGAN INNINGS

R.D.B. Croft	c Lewis	b Harvey	11
M.T.G. Elliott		b Harvey	9
M.J. Powell	c and	b Snape	48
*M.P. Maynard	run out		104
A. Dale	run out		5
S.P. James		b Averis	7
K. Newell	c Cunliffe	b Harvey	1
+A.D. Shaw	c Barnett	b Averis	1
A.G. Wharf	lbw	b Harvey	8
S.L. Watkin		b Harvey	10
O.T. Parkin		not out	0
Extras		(LB 5, W 8, NB 8)	21
Total			**225**

FOW: 1-18, 2-24, 3-161, 4-178, 5-192,
6-195, 7-202, 8-213, 9-225

Bowling	O	M	R	W
Harvey	9.3	1	34	5
Smith	10	1	44	0
Lewis	5	0	23	0
Averis	10	0	49	2
Alleyne	7	0	33	0
Snape	8	0	37	1

GLOUCESTERSHIRE INNINGS

T.H.C. Hancock	c and	b Parkin	60
K.J. Barnett		b Croft	39
R.J. Cunliffe	c Shaw	b Watkin	24
M.G.N. Windows	not out		53
*M.W. Alleyne	not out		40
Extras		(B 1, LB 4, W 3, NB 2)	10
Total		(for 3 wickets)	**226**

DNB: I.J. Harvey, J.N. Snape, +R.C. Russell, J. Lewis, J.M.M. Averis,
A.M. Smith.
FOW: 1-80, 2-118, 3-131

Bowling	O	M	R	W
Parkin	8	1	46	1
Watkin	10	1	42	1
Wharf	10	0	48	0
Croft	10	0	39	1
Dale	8.5	0	46	0

Gloucestershire won by 7 wickets

SUSSEX

22, 23, 24, 25 August 2000 at Colwyn Bay

This collection of classic matches finishes with a truly amazing game from 2000, when Glamorgan played Sussex at the delightful Rhos ground at Colwyn Bay. Since the mid-1960s, Glamorgan have regularly travelled up to the popular resort in order to fly the county flag and to reward their loyal supporters in North Wales. The wicket at the Rhos ground has generally been one on which the batsmen have gorged themselves, but in the 1999 match with Nottinghamshire, the wicket had displayed a more capricious character on the first morning, as the visitors were reduced to 9-6 after six overs. Perhaps these events from the previous year were in the minds of both captains on the morning of this game in 2000. Both were thinking about bowling first and, having won the toss, it was Chris Adams who had to decide. He duly invited Glamorgan to take first use of a green looking wicket, but then saw the home side reach 457-1 by the close of play, with Steve James and Matt Elliott adding a record 374 for the first wicket.

It was not the first time that James had found Colwyn Bay to be a happy hunting ground, having made 259* against Nottinghamshire in 1999 and 162 against the same opponents in 1997. This match saw James continue his productive sequence and inflict further punishment on the weary Sussex bowlers, as he recorded the first ever triple hundred in Glamorgan's history, reaching this landmark after lunch on the second day with a late cut off Umer Rashid.

His steadfast and stylish innings also saw the Glamorgan batsmen rewrite their record book with a total of 718-3 – the highest innings total in the club's history. When Matthew Maynard declared seventy minutes into the afternoon session, it ended an innings that had also seen every partnership against the beleaguered Sussex bowlers yield over a hundred runs.

The visitors were naturally quite weary after a day and a half of leather chasing, and they did quite well to amass 342 – a total that in a normal game would have been sufficient to avoid the follow-on. Captain Adams hit a gallant 156, whilst Rashid scored a maiden Championship hundred during a spirited partnership of 232 for the sixth wicket. But even this was not enough to prevent Sussex from following-on and, after some hostile bowling and five wickets from Alex Wharf, Sussex batted again, some 376 runs behind.

Within eight overs, both of their openers were back in the pavilion and, although Adams and Robin Martin-Jenkins both offered valiant resistance, it was really only a matter of time before Glamorgan were able to celebrate victory. In the end, it was Adrian Dale who hastened Sussex's demise, with a return of 5 for 46. As the Sussex players headed home after lunch on the fourth day, they must have been wondering how many other counties had scored over 300 in each innings, yet still lost by an innings.

Matthew Elliott hits a boundary during his century at Colwyn Bay .

Steve James batting at Colwyn Bay in 1999 during his double-century against Nottinghamshire.

GLAMORGAN 1ST INNINGS

M.T.G. Elliott		b Kirtley	177
S.P. James	not out		309
M.J. Powell		b Kirtley	64
*+M.P. Maynard		b House	67
A. Dale	not out		48
K. Newell			
R.D.B. Croft			
S.D. Thomas			
A.G. Wharf			
D.A. Cosker			
S.L. Watkin			
Extras	(B 12, LB 13, W 8, NB 20)		53
Total	(for 3 wickets dec)		**718**

FOW:1-374, 2-497, 3-631

Bowling	O	M	R	W
Lewry	29	3	131	0
Kirtley	40	5	169	2
Martin-Jenkins	22	2	117	0
Robinson	30	4	111	0
Rashid	24	3	111	0
Yardy	5	0	17	0
House	10	0	34	1
Adams	2	0	3	0

SUSSEX   1ST INNINGS / 2ND INNINGS

	1ST INNINGS			2ND INNINGS		
R.R. Montgomerie	c Maynard	b Cosker	23	c Powell	b Watkin	6
M.H. Yardy		b Wharf	4		b Wharf	9
P.A. Cottey	c Maynard	b Wharf	2	c sub	b Watkin	2
*C.J. Adams	c Cosker	b Wharf	156	lbw	b Wharf	68
W.J. House	c Croft	b Watkin	0	lbw	b Dale	13
R.S.C. Martin-Jenkins	c sub	b Watkin	8		b Dale	77
U.B.A. Rashid	c Croft	b Watkin	110	c Wharf	b Dale	54
+N.J. Wilton	c James	b Wharf	15	not out		32
R.J. Kirtley	c Maynard	b Watkin	4		b Dale	12
J.D. Lewry	not out		1		b Dale	4
M.A. Robinson		b Wharf	0		b Croft	2
Extras	(LB 5, NB 14)		19	(B 4, LB 15,NB 18)		37
Total			**342**			**316**

FOW: 1-9, 2-11, 3-77, 4-78, 5-86,   1-19, 2-21, 3-26, 4-50, 5-176,
6-318, 7-322, 8-336, 9-342   6-260, 7-267, 8-293, 9-305

Bowling	O	M	R	W	Bowling	O	M	R	W
Wharf	16.5	3	68	5	Wharf	9	0	65	2
Watkin	26	7	76	4	Watkin	15	4	45	2
Thomas	21	5	69	0	Thomas	15	2	72	0
Croft	25	5	77	0	Croft	14.5	2	42	1
Cosker	18	9	43	1	Cosker	7	0	27	0
Dale	2	1	4	0	Dale	16	4	46	5

Glamorgan won by an innings and 60 runs

Steve James and Matthew Elliott proudly stand in front of the Colwyn Bay scoreboard after their record opening stand.